MW00381074

Mediterranean Diet

── Slow Cooker ──

Cookbook

100 Vibrant, Family-Approved Recipes to Save Time and Have a
Healthier Body

Bernice Thurman

Contents

Introduction

The Mediterranean diet has become quite a popular option for people who want to enjoy the benefits that come with plant-based foods today. The diet has gained attention from scientific experts and researchers from all regions of the world. Many studies have already been conducted to understand the benefits that may come with a Mediterranean diet.

People who follow a Mediterranean diet have been found to have a lower risk of heart disease, inflammation, and reduced body weight. Blood sugar is also seemingly regulated by following this type of diet.

Preparation of meals that are suitable for a Mediterranean diet can sometimes take some time. This is why it is not uncommon to see people who follow this particular diet use an slow cooker. These devices make preparing meals much more simple and easier. At the same time, they also provide added benefits when following a Mediterranean diet.

In this book, we look at what the Mediterranean diet is. We also take a brief look at the history of the diet. The post considers the many health benefits that have been associated with the diet. Additionally, we also look at the benefits that may come with using a slow cooker to prepare meals while following the Mediterranean diet.

Chapter 1

ALL YOU NEED TO KNOW ABOUT MEDITERRANEAN DIET

The History Of The Mediterranean Diet

The Mediterranean diet is based on eating habits from multiple cultures. The diet was initially published by a husband and wife team. Biologist Ancel Keys and Markaret Keys, a chemist, worked together in order to develop a diet that focuses on providing a combination of different eating habits into one diet. It was first made public in 1975.

The diet essentially takes from eating habits related to Italy and Greece. The eating habits contained within the Mediterranean diet were very popular in these two countries within the 1960s.

During the early stages, after the diet was made public, it failed to gain much attention. In the 1990s, however, the diet quickly gained recognition. People quickly started to adopt the diet, particularly due to the health claims made by the authors.
Researchers took note of the Mediterranean diet and started to conduct studies. These studies quickly made the world aware of the health benefits that may come with the eating habits introduced by Ancel Keys and Markaret Keys.

Why The Mediterranean Diet?

The Mediterranean diet focuses on teaching us how to intake more fresh vegetables and fruits in our diet and with that introducing all the vital vitamins and minerals that our body requires. And while you are supposed to eat red meat on only rare occasions, fish and seafood are a must. Eggs, yogurt, milk, and cheese are also welcomed but in moderation. Sweets, artificial sweeteners, processed meat, and highly processed foods have no place in the Mediterranean diet.

The Mediterranean diet has been reported to have many health benefits.
- Improved cardiovascular health
- Reduced risk of health disease and heart attack
- Low cholesterol levels
- Reduced risk of hypertension
- Reduced risk of stroke
- Reduced risk of diabetes mellitus and improved condition among those with diabetes mellitus
- Weight loss
- Reduced facial wrinkles, dark spots on the skin

Studies On The Mediterranean Diet

A large number of scientific studies have been conducted on the Mediterranean diet to date. Many of these studies had shown positive effects when the diet was adopted by people with certain diseases. Additionally, the diet is also a great choice for promoting general health. People who follow a Mediterranean diet seem to complain less about certain diseases and disorders.

To provide a better view of the benefits that the diet may offer, we need to turn our focus toward studies published on the topic.

A large study involved a total of 7,447 participants. The published paper was termed the "PREDIMED Study." All of the individuals who took part in the study had high-risk factors linked to heart disease. Three diets were used among the participants. This was also a long-term study, lasting for a period of five years.

A control group was introduced, who was offered a low-fat diet. The other two groups both consumed meals that were in line with the Mediterranean diet. The one group was instructed to follow a Mediterranean diet with extra virgin olive oil, while the other group followed the diet with additional nuts added.

The study was divided into multiple sections. Various results were obtained, but the majority of findings pointed toward positive effects related to the Mediterranean diet.

There was a 31% reduction in the risk of

heart disease in the group who consumed a Mediterranean diet with extra virgin olive oil. Among those with extra nuts, a 28% reduction in the risk for death from heart-related events were noted. Similar results were not noted among the participants part of the control group.

In one study, it was shown that the Mediterranean diet provided effective results within as short of a period as three months. There was a reduction in various cardiovascular risk factors noted when participants were provided this diet for a 90-day period.

Improvements were found in the following vitals and measurements:
- Blood sugar levels
- Systolic blood pressure levels
- Total cholesterol and cholesterol ratio
- C-reactive protein levels

In another study, it was shown that the Mediterranean diet might also be highly effective at helping a person with weight management. Total cholesterol, weight, and endothelial function score were recorded among participants.

Among those who followed a Mediterranean diet, there was an average reduction of 8.8 pounds in body weight. Among those who were part of a low-fat control group, the average weight reduction was recorded as 2.6 pounds.

The Mediterranean diet also provided a significant improvement in Endothelial function among the participants. Such an improvement was not noted among the people who were part of a control group.

In addition to these findings, researchers also noted a reduction in insulin resistance markings. Inflammatory markers among the participants who followed a Mediterranean diet were also reduced.

Mediterranean Diet Rules

To experience the health benefits associated with the Mediterranean diet, it is important for a person to understand the rules that come with this eating style. The diet is not very strict, but there are a few important rules to comply with. By following through with all these rules, there is a greater chance of experiencing the benefits that scientific studies have linked to a Mediterranean diet.

The primary rule of the Mediterranean diet is to adopt eating habits that prioritize plant-based foods instead of meat-based foods. The majority of foods that are included in the diet are of plant-based origin.

Even though plant-based foods are prioritized, it should be noted that it does not mean a person can never eat other foods. Some alternative foods are allowed in moderation or occasionally. Eating too much of the foods that should only be included occasionally can, however, reduce the benefits that the diet is able to offer a person.

Here is the basic structure of the Mediterranean diet:
  Foundation: Plant-based foods
  Moderate: Seafood, poultry, eggs, and dairy
  Occasionally: Red meat

Foods You Can Eat

There are a lot of foods that can be included in a Mediterranean diet – but you should make sure you to understand the specifics.

The main foods that are generally considered an important part of the diet include those that are processed from plant sources. Examples of these include:
  Vegetables and fruit (Up to 10 servings per day)
  Nuts
  Beans
  Whole grains
  Herbs
  Spices

These are the primary foods that meals are built around – additional foods in other categories can then be added at specific occasions.

Red wine can also be consumed, but only in moderation.

People who eat a lot of bread should make a few changes. When following a Mediterranean diet, white bread should be switched out for whole wheat bread. There are also whole grain options when looking at pasta and pizza dough. These are excellent alternatives.

Fruit juice can be consumed, but not in excess amounts. An unsweetened fruit juice still contains a lot of sugars. Sugar is something that is generally avoided as much as possible on a Mediterranean diet.

Foods To Avoid

While there are quite a few foods that can be included in a Mediterranean diet, people also need to be aware of what they should not include. There are many foods that can interfere with the diet's ability to offer the body the claimed benefits.

Some of the most important foods to avoid when following a Mediterranean diet include:
- Hot dogs
- Processed meat products
- Deli meat products
- Refined grains (white pasta, pizza dough made with white flour, and white bread)
- Food that contains a lot of added sugar (soda, candy, and pastries)
- Refined oils (Soybean oil and canola oil are examples)

Chapter 2

YOUR IN-DEPTH SLOW COOKER GUIDE FOR DELICIOUS DISHES

Slow Cookers are also called slow cookers. They are considered as a great time-saving kitchen device that is great for all types of cooks but most especially those who are novice in the kitchen. With this device, you can put every ingredient in the pot, turn it on and wait for it to cook hours later. This means that you can prepare dinner in the morning and expect it to be done and piping hot once you get back home in the evening.

Cooking with Slow Cookers may be very easy but there are certain things that you need to know so that you can create delicious dishes out of this humble kitchen appliance. Thus, this chapter is dedicated to what you need to know about Slow Cookers so that you can optimize its uses.

The Benefits of Using a Slow Cooker

Cooking with a slow cooker is one of the best ways to save time as well as prepare delicious and nutritious meals. With a slow cooker, you can put your ingredients in the pot and it cooks the entire day slowly so that it becomes ready by the time you get back. Aside from convenience, there are also other benefits of using a Slow Cooker. Below are the benefits of using a Slow Cooker.

● **Mess-free:** Cooking with a Slow Cooker is mess-free. The thing is that there are no dishes or cups that you need to clean as you pot all ingredients in the pot and you are good to go. Clean up of the Slow Cooker is also a breeze as you can wipe it with a clean kitchen towel. You can also line heat-proof plastic in the Slow Cooker so that the interior of the pot remains clean.

● **It requires less electricity:** To cook your food, Slow Cookers do not require large amount of electricity to be able to do its work. Since it does not use a lot of energy, it does not also heat up your entire kitchen space compared to when you use an oven.

● **Use cheaper cuts of meat:** The condensation that occurs in the Slow Cookers serve as self-basting machines thus cheaper cuts of meat become tender if cooked in a slow cooker.

● **Cooks flavorful dishes:** And since you can use cheaper cuts of meat in a Slow Cooker, it does not mean that your food will become less tasty. In fact, vegetables that are cooked in a Slow Cooker absorbs the flavor of the spices and the stock.

● **Allows you to adjust the temperature:** Slow Cookers come with both high and low settings so you can adjust the temperature as well as the cooking time of your food. If you are at home and you want to sauté or simmer your food faster, the high setting is perfect but if you want to leave your food to cook by itself, you need to select the low setting.

How Does It Work?

What makes Slow Cookers great is that they simplify the cooking process so that you can prepare meals even if you have limited cooking skills or if you are cooking your way through your busy schedule. But how does it work? The thing is that understanding how Slow Cookers work is essential so that you will be able to cook delicious food no matter what.

The success of the Slow Cooker in slow cooking your food relies on its design. Slow Cookers are basically electric pots that come with stoneware inserts. So unlike conventional stove top cooking, slow cookers can consistently cook food at low temperature for 12 hours. The stoneware inserts trap heat thus it can cook food for a long period of time.

As a general rule, Slow Cookers cook food under low temperature setting of 190 0F or 87 0C, which is under the boiling point temperature. Under the high setting, food is cooked at 250 0F or 121 0C.

However, there are other brands that offer other temperature ranges so you have to choose the ones that you are comfortable working with. But if you are in doubt, stick with this temperature setting.

Food is cooked in its own juices for a period of several hours thus the dish embodies the rich and natural flavors of the ingredients. Moreover, the use of low heat to cook food steadily brings out the flavor of food giving the final dish extra richness.

You cook food by layering different ingredients on the pot and cooking them for a few hours until they are done. The cooking time varies from one dish to another. As a general rule, side dishes as well as desserts can cook between 4 to 6 hours while meat dishes can take longer for about 6 to 10 hours. Some of the Slow Cookers also feature a high temperature setting so that foods can be cooked between 3 and 4 hours.

General Cooking Tips

Just like other types of cooking appliances, there are some things that you need to know about Slow Cookers so that you can cook delicious food even if it is your first time using it. Below are the general cooking tips that you need to know by heart when using your Slow Cooker.

● **Cook just enough:** Fill the Slow Cooker with ½ to ¾ full of ingredients including liquid. The thing is that your food will not cook through if it is full to the brim. On the other hand, if the food level is lower than recommended, it may lead to your food cooking quickly thus resulting to burning.

● **Place dry ingredients at the bottom:** The ingredients placed at the bottom of the Slow Cooker cooks faster than those placed on top. Moreover, ingredients at the bottom also have more moisture than ingredients at the top because they are soaked in the simmering liquid. Thus said, place ingredients that are dry at the bottom of the Slow Cooker.

- **Meat requires at least 8 hours of cooking:** Most meats from poultry to beef requires at least 8 hours of cooking. You can use different types of meat cuts and they will cook moist and tender after 8 hours.

- **Remove skin and fat from meats:** Whether you are cooking poultry or red meat, it is recommended that you remove skin and fat from meat. The thing is that fat melts if subjected to long cooking time thus it adds an unpleasant texture to the dish. Moreover, fats also cook the food quickly thus it may lead to having a dry texture if cooked for a long time in a slow cooker.

- **Always follow the layering instructions of ingredients:** While there is no specific layering instruction that you can follow, you need to cook the vegetables at the bottom while the meat should be on top where it is nearer the heating element.

- **Never lift the lid while cooking on low setting:** You don't need to stir your food if you are cooking in the low setting thus there is no need to lift the lid. The thing is that every time you lift the lid, heat will escape from the pot thus affecting the cooking time such that you need to extend to a few minutes to cook your food. Checking the progress of your food is easy as the Slow Cooker comes with a glass lid. You just need to spin the cover without removing it from the pot to remove the condensation so that you can see your food inside the pot.

- **Use the high setting to thicken sauces:** If you are planning on adding thickeners, opt for the high setting during the last hour of the cooking time and add the cornstarch slurry. Stir the liquid to evenly thicken the sauce and wait for 15 minutes.

Slow Cooker Safety Tips

Slow cookers are designed to cook food for a few hours at a time by heating food properly at low temperature. Food is cooked at a low temperature which may lead bacterial colonies to populate your food. Thus, it is important that your food is fully cooked within 4 hours to avoid harboring bad bacteria. To avoid problems regarding the possible spoiling of food, below are Slow Cooker safety tips that you need to be aware of and put into practice.

- **Ensure that the work area is clean:** Make sure that the work area around your Slow Cooker is clear to avoid contamination of your food.

- **Prepare meat and veggies separately:** If you are preparing meat and vegetables beforehand, make sure that you prepare and store them separately to avoid cross-contamination.

- **Thaw the meat before putting in the slow cooker:** Defrost your meats so that they will cook all the way through the cooking duration. Moreover, it also allows the meat to achieve safe internal temperature thus preventing the risk of food poisoning.

- **Pay attention to the temperature:** It is crucial that the Slow Cooker reaches a temperature that will effectively kill bacteria. You can start with the highest temperature setting for an hour and switch to low for the remaining cooking time. Although this may be the case, it is still safe to cook food at low temperature especially if you have to leave for work. Just use a food thermometer to check the internal temperature of your meat to see if it is cooked through.

Make sure that your food fits inside the pot: Never fill the Slow Cooker full to the brim. To effectively cook your food, the pot should be filled with ½ or ¾ full.

Cut up your meat: Cut your meat up before putting them in the slow cooker so that they do not cook for a long time as well as they cook all the way through the meat.

POULTRY RECIPES

Family Dinner Chicken

 Servings: 6   **Cooking Time: 4 hours**   **Preparation Time: 20 minutes**

Nutrition Information:

Calories per serving: 630; Carbohydrates: 8g; Protein: 88.5g; Fat: 25.1g; Sugar: 3.2g; Sodium: 95mg; Fiber: 2.3g

Ingredients:

- 1 tbsp. olive oil
- 1 tbsp. fresh lemon juice
- 3 garlic cloves, minced
- 1 tsp. dried thyme
- 1 tbsp. paprika
- 1 tsp. garlic powder
- 1 tsp. ground cumin
- ½ tsp. ground cinnamon
- ½ tsp. cayenne pepper
- 1 (4-lb.) whole chicken, neck and giblets removed
- 4 carrots, peeled and cut into large chunks
- 2 celery stalks, cut into large chunks
- 1 medium sweet onion, cut into large chunks
- 1 garlic clove, sliced
- ½ lemon, sliced
- 2 bay leaves

Instructions:

1) In a small bowl, mix together the olive oil and lemon juice. Set aside.
2) In another bowl, mix together the minced garlic, thyme and spices.
3) Brush the chicken with oil mixture and then rub with spice mixture generously.
4) Stuff the cavity of chicken with garlic slices, lemon slices and bay leaves.
5) In a greased slow cooker, place the carrots, celery and onion chunks.
6) Place the chicken on top of the vegetables.
7) Set the slow cooker on "High" and cook, covered for about 3-4 hours.
8) Remove from the slow cooker and place the chicken onto a cutting board for about 10 minutes.
9) Cut the chicken into desired sized pieces and serve alongside the vegetables.

Festive Entrée Chicken

 Servings: 6   **Cooking Time: 7 hours 27 minutes** **Preparation Time: 15 minutes**

Nutrition Information:

Calories per serving: 183; Carbohydrates: 9.1g;
Protein: 27.4g; Fat: 4.2g; Sugar: 0.9g; Sodium:
88mg; Fiber: 2.9g

Ingredients:

- 1½ lb. skinless, boneless chicken breast halves
- 1 (9-oz.) package frozen artichoke hearts
- ½ C. onion, chopped
- 12 garlic cloves, minced
- ½ C. low-sodium chicken broth
- 2 tsp. dried rosemary, crushed
- 1 tsp. lemon zest, grated finely
- ½ tsp. ground black pepper
- 1 tbsp. cornstarch
- 1 tbsp. cold water

Instructions:

1) Heat a large non-stick skillet over medium heat and cook the chicken breast halves in 2 batches for about 2-3 minutes per side or until browned.
2) In the bottom of a slow cooker, mix together the artichoke hearts, onion, garlic, broth, rosemary, lemon zest and black pepper.
3) Arrange the browned chicken on top in a single layer.
4) Place some of the garlic mixture over chicken.
5) Set the slow cooker on "Low" and cook, covered for about 6-7 hours.
6) With a slotted spoon, transfer the chicken and artichokes onto a platter.
7) With a piece of foil, cover the chicken and artichokes to keep warm.
8) In a small bowl, dissolve the cornstarch into water.
9) Set the slow cooker on "High" and stir in the cornstarch mixture, stirring continuously.
10) Cook, covered for about 15 minutes.
11) Place the sauce over chicken and artichokes and serve.

Restaurant Worthy Chicken

 Servings: 6   **Cooking Time: 5 hours 10 minutes** **Preparation Time: 15 minutes**

Nutrition Information:

Calories per serving: 357; Carbohydrates: 6.1g; Protein: 45g; Fat: 16.2g; Sugar: 2.3g; Sodium: 34mg; Fiber: 1.8g

Ingredients:

- 1 tbsp. olive oil
- 2 lb. boneless, skinless chicken thighs
- 1 sweet onion, sliced thinly
- 3 garlic cloves, minced
- 1 C. roasted red peppers, chopped
- 1 C. olives
- ½ C. chicken broth
- 1 tbsp. capers
- 1 bay leaf
- 1 tsp. rosemary
- 1 tsp. dried thyme
- 1 tsp. dried oregano
- Salt and freshly ground black pepper, to taste
- 2 tbsp. fresh lemon juice

Instructions:

1) In a skillet, heat the oil over medium-high heat and cook the chicken thighs for about 4-5 minutes per side or until browned.
2) With a slotted spoon, transfer the chicken thighs onto a plate.
3) In the same skillet, add the onion and garlic and sauté for about 4-5 minutes.
4) In a slow cooker, add the cooked chicken thighs, onion mixture and remaining ingredients except for lemon juice and stir to combine.
5) Set the slow cooker on "Low" and cook, covered for about 4-5 hours.
6) Drizzle with lemon juice and serve.

►► Classic Chicken Cacciatore

 Servings: 6   **Cooking Time: 8 hours**   **Preparation Time: 15 minutes**

Nutrition Information:

Calories per serving: 368; Carbohydrates: 15.8g;
Protein: 49.2g; Fat: 11.6g; Sugar: 10.2g; Sodium:
705mg; Fiber: 5.5g

Ingredients:

- 2 lb. skin-on, bone-in chicken thighs
- Salt and freshly ground black pepper, to taste
- 2 bell peppers, seeded and chopped
- 8 oz. fresh baby Bella mushrooms, sliced
- 2 garlic cloves, minced
- 1 (28-oz.) can crushed tomatoes
- ½ C. chicken broth
- 1 tsp. dried oregano
- ¼ tsp. red pepper flakes
- 1/3 C. capers

Instructions:

1) Season the chicken with salt and black pepper evenly.
2) In a slow cooker, place all ingredients except for capers and stir to combine.
3) Set the slow cooker on "High" and cook, covered for about 6-8 hours.
4) Uncover the slow cooker and stir in the capers.
5) Serve hot.

Chicken Ragout

 Servings: 8 **Cooking Time: 4 hours 55 minutes** **Preparation Time: 15 minutes**

Nutrition Information:

Calories per serving: 323; Carbohydrates: 17.5g;
Protein: 37.9g; Fat: 10.g; Sugar: 3.9g; Sodium:
40mg; Fiber: 4.9g

Ingredients:

- 1 lb. carrots, peeled and cut into 1¼-inch pieces
- 1 lb. Yukon Gold potatoes, peeled and cut into wide wedges
- 2 lb. boneless, skinless chicken thighs, trimmed
- 1 (14-oz.) can low-sodium chicken broth
- 1/3 C. dry white wine
- 4 garlic cloves, minced
- Salt, to taste
- 1 (15-oz.) can artichoke hearts, rinsed and quartered
- 1 large egg
- 2 large egg yolks
- 1/3 C. fresh lemon juice
- 1/3 C. fresh dill, chopped
- Freshly ground black pepper, to taste

Instructions:

1) In the bottom of a slow cooker, place the carrots and potatoes and arrange the chicken thighs on top.
2) Ina small saucepan, add the broth, wine, garlic and salt over medium-high heat and bring to a boil.
3) Remove from the heat and pour the broth mister over chicken mixture.
4) Set the slow cooker on "Low" and cook, covered for about 4-4½ hours.
5) Remove the cover and place the artichokes into the slow cooker.
6) Set the slow cooker on "High" and cook, covered for about 5 minutes.
7) Meanwhile, in a bowl, add the egg, egg yolks and lemon juice and beat well.
8) Remove the cover and with a slotted spoon, transfer the chicken and vegetables into a serving bowl.
9) With a slotted spoon, cover the bowl to keep warm.
10) Place about ½ C. of the cooking liquid into the egg mixture and beat until smooth.
11) Slowly, add the egg mixture into the remaining cooking liquid in the slow cooker, beating continuously.
12) Set the slow cooker on "High" and cook, covered for about 15-20 minutes, beating 2-3 times.
13) Remove the cover and stir in the dill and black pepper.
14) Place the sauce over the chicken and vegetables and serve.

►► Budget-Friendly Chicken Platter

 **Servings: 8** **Cooking Time: 5 hours** **Preparation Time: 15 minutes**

Nutrition Information:

Calories per serving: 392; Carbohydrates: 48.2g;
Protein: 35.7g; Fat: 6.3g; Sugar: 8.7g; Sodium:
109mg; Fiber: 12.3g

Ingredients:

- 2 lb. boneless, skinless chicken breast
- 2 large sweet potatoes, peeled and chopped
- 1 onion, chopped
- 2 garlic cloves, minced
- 2 large carrots, peeled and chopped
- 1 (15 oz.) can chickpeas, rinsed and drained
- 1 (14½-oz.) can diced tomatoes with juices
- 1 tsp. dried parsley
- ½ tsp. ground turmeric
- ½ tsp. ground cumin
- ¼ tsp. ground cinnamon
- Salt and freshly ground black pepper, to taste

Instructions:

1) In a slow cooker, place all the ingredients and stir to combine.
2) Set the slow cooker on "High" and cook, covered for about 4-5 hours.
3) Serve hot.

 # Wonderfully Flavored Chicken

 Servings: 4   **Cooking Time: 6 hours 40 minutes**   **Preparation Time: 15 minutes**

Nutrition Information:

Calories per serving: 445; Carbohydrates: 8.9g;
Protein: 35.7g; Fat: 31.2g; Sugar: 2.1g; Sodium:
24mg; Fiber: 1.2g

Ingredients:

- 12 pepperoncini peppers, rinsed and drained
- 1 C. Kalamata olives, pitted and sliced
- 8 garlic cloves, minced
- 3½ lb. chicken leg quarters
- 1½ tsp. paprika
- Salt and freshly ground black pepper, to taste
- ½ tsp. lemon zest, grated
- ½ C. fresh lemon juice
- 1 C. sour cream

Instructions:

1) In the bottom of a slow cooker, place the pepperoncini, followed by the olive slices, garlic and chicken leg quarters.
2) Sprinkle with paprika, salt, black pepper and lemon zest.
3) Drizzle with lemon juice.
4) Set the slow cooker on "Low" and cook, covered for about 6-6½ hours.
5) With a slotted spoon, transfer the chicken leg quarters onto a platter.
6) With a piece of foil, cover the chicken leg quarters to keep warm.
7) Set the slow cooker on "High" and with a slotted spoon, skim off the fat from cooking liquid.
8) Add the sour cream, beating continuously until well combined.
9) Cook, covered for about 8-10 minutes.
10) Pour hot sauce over chicken and serve.

Weeknight Dinner Meal

 **Servings: 6** **Cooking Time: 4 ¾ hours** **Preparation Time: 15 minutes**

Nutrition Information:

Calories per serving: 708; Carbohydrates: 12.4g; Protein: 91.2g; Fat: 29.8g; Sugar: 2g; Sodium: 672mg; Fiber: 4.9g

Ingredients:	Instructions:

Ingredients:

- 1 (4-5-lb.) cut-up skinless whole chicken
- Salt and freshly ground black pepper, to taste
- 2 tbsp. olive oil
- ½ C. dry white wine
- 6 thin lemon slices
- 1 large red onion, cut into wedges
- 5 garlic cloves, chopped finely
- 1 tsp. Herbes de Provence
- 1 C. chicken broth
- 1 (14-oz.) can quartered artichoke hearts, drained
- 30 pimiento-stuffed manzanilla olives
- ¼ C. fresh Italian flat-leaf parsley, chopped

Instructions:

1) Season the chicken pieces with salt and black pepper evenly.
2) In skillet, heat the oil over medium-high heat and cook the chicken pieces in 2 batches for about 4-6 minutes, flipping once halfway through.
3) Place the chicken pieces in a greased slow cooker.
4) In the same skillet, add the wine over medium heat and cook for about 2-3 minutes, scraping up the browned bits from the bottom.
5) Remove from the heat and place the wine over chicken.
6) Place the lemon slices over chicken, followed by the onion, garlic, and Herbes de Provence.
7) Top with the broth.
8) Set the slow cooker on "Low" and cook, covered for about 4 hours.
9) Remove the cover and stir in the artichoke hearts and olives.
10) Set the slow cooker on "Low" and cook, covered for about 30 minutes.
11) Serve with the garnishing of parsley.

▶▶ Brightly Flavored Chicken

 Servings: 6　 **Cooking Time: 2 hours 4 minutes**　 **Preparation Time: 20 minutes**

Nutrition Information:

Calories per serving: 397; Carbohydrates: 8.8g; Protein: 46.6g; Fat: 18.8g; Sugar: 4.8g; Sodium: 28mg; Fiber: 2g

Ingredients:

- 2 lb. boneless, skinless chicken breasts
- Salt and freshly ground black pepper, to taste
- 1 tbsp. extra-virgin olive oil
- 1 (12 oz.) jar roasted red peppers, drained and chopped
- 1 medium red onion, cut into ½-inch chunks
- 1 C. Kalamata olives
- 3 tbsp. red wine vinegar
- 1 tsp. honey
- 1 tbsp. garlic, minced
- 1 tsp. dried oregano
- 1 tsp. dried thyme
- ½ C. feta cheese, crumbled
- 2 tbsp. fresh thyme, chopped

Instructions:

1) Season the chicken with salt and black pepper evenly.
2) In a large skillet, heat the oil over medium-high heat and cook the chicken breasts for about 1-2 minutes per side.
3) Transfer the chicken breast into a greased slow cooker.
4) Arrange the peppers, onions and olives around the chicken breasts.
5) In a small bowl, add the vinegar, honey, garlic and dried herbs and beat until well combined.
6) Place the vinegar mixture over the chicken and vegetables.
7) Set the slow cooker on "High" and cook, covered for about 1½-2 hours.
8) Serve with the topping of feta and thyme.

 # Luscious Stuffed Chicken

 Servings: 6   **Cooking Time: 6 hours**   **Preparation Time: 20 minutes**

Nutrition Information:

Calories per serving: 370; Carbohydrates: 6.2g;
Protein: 48.5g; Fat: 16.1g; Sugar: 2g; Sodium:
556mg; Fiber: 2.4g

Ingredients:

- 3 C. fresh spinach, chopped finely
- 1 C. artichoke hearts, chopped
- ½ C. roasted red peppers, chopped
- ¼ C. black olives, sliced
- 4 oz. feta cheese, crumbled
- 1 tsp. dried oregano
- 1 tsp. garlic powder
- ½ C. chicken broth
- 2 lb. boneless, skinless chicken breasts
- Salt and freshly ground black pepper, to taste

Instructions:

1) In a bowl, add the vegetables, feta, oregano and garlic powder and mix well. Set aside.
2) With a small, sharp knife make a deep cut in each chicken breast to make a pocket. (Be careful not to cut through the chicken).
3) Season chicken breast with salt and black pepper generously.
4) Stuff each chicken breast with veggie mixture.
5) In the bottom of a slow cooker, add the broth.
6) Now, place the chicken breasts in the slow cooker, cut side should be facing up.
7) Set the slow cooker on "Low" and cook, covered for about 4-6 hours.
8) Serve hot.

Creamy Chicken Milano

Servings: 8   **Cooking Time: 5 hours**   **Preparation Time: 15 minutes**

Nutrition Information:

Calories per serving: 421; Carbohydrates: 9.1g; Protein: 51.3g; Fat: 20.4g; Sugar: 1.6g; Sodium: 500mg; Fiber: 1.4g

Ingredients:	Instructions:

Ingredients:

- 3 lb. chicken tenderloins
- Salt and freshly ground black pepper, to taste
- 16 oz. fresh Cremini mushrooms, sliced
- 3½ tbsp. fresh basil, chopped
- 8 oz. cream cheese, softened
- 10½ oz. cream of chicken soup with herbs
- 10½ oz. cream of mushroom soup with roasted garlic
- ½ C. chicken broth
- 1 lb. ham slices
- 2 C. mozzarella cheese, shredded
- ¼ C. fresh parsley, chopped

Instructions:

1) Season the chicken tenderloins with salt and black pepper generously.
2) In the bottom of a slow cooker, place the chicken tenderloins, followed by the mushrooms and basil.
3) In a bowl, add the cream cheese, cream soups and broth and with an electric mixer, mix for about 2-4 minutes cream cheese mixture on top of mushrooms.
4) Arrange the ham slices on top and sprinkle with the mozzarella cheese.
5) Set the slow cooker on "Low" and cook, covered for about 4-5 hours.
6) Serve with the garnishing of parsley.

►► Versatile Chicken Dinner

 **Servings: 8** **Cooking Time: 8 hours 6 minutes** **Preparation Time: 15 minutes**

Nutrition Information:

Calories per serving: 497; Carbohydrates: 18.7g; Protein: 55.5g; Fat: 21.6g; Sugar: 1.2g; Sodium: 280mg; Fiber: 2.1g

Ingredients:

- ½ tsp. dried oregano
- ½ tsp. dried basil
- ¼ tsp. dried rosemary
- Salt and freshly ground black pepper, to taste
- 8 bone-in, skin-on chicken thighs
- 2 tbsp. unsalted butter
- 2 lb. baby red potatoes, quartered
- 2 tbsp. olive oil
- 4 garlic cloves, minced
- ½ tsp. dried thyme
- 1 C. Parmesan cheese, grated
- 2 tbsp. fresh parsley, chopped

Instructions:

1) In a bowl, add the oregano, basil, rosemary, salt and black pepper and mix well.
2) Season the chicken thighs with herb mixture generously.
3) In a large skillet, melt the butter over medium-high heat.
4) Place the chicken thighs, skin-side down and cook for about 2-3 minutes.
5) Flip and cook for about 2-3 minutes.
6) In a greased slow cooker, place the potatoes and stir in the oil, garlic and thyme, salt and black pepper.
7) Arrange the chicken thighs on top in an even layer.
8) Set the slow cooker on "Low" and cook, covered for about 7-8 hours.
9) Top with Parmesan and parsley and serve immediately.

►► Absolutely Delicious Chicken

 Servings: 6   Cooking Time: 4 ½ hours   Preparation Time: 15 minutes

Nutrition Information:

Calories per serving: 310; Carbohydrates: 9.1g; Protein: 43.7g; Fat: 10.7g; Sugar: 1.2g; Sodium: 17mg; Fiber: 4.3g

Ingredients:	Instructions:

Ingredients:

- ½ tbsp. dried oregano
- ½ tsp. smoked paprika
- Salt and freshly ground black pepper, to taste
- 6 boneless, skinless chicken thighs
- 1 (14¾-oz.) jar grilled artichoke hearts, drained,
- 4 garlic cloves, minced
- 1/3 C. liquid from artichoke hearts
- 1 (3½-oz.) julienned sun-dried tomatoes
- 3 tbsp. fresh parsley, chopped

Instructions:

1) In a small bowl, mix together the oregano, paprika, salt and black pepper.
2) Season the chicken thighs with thyme mixture evenly.
3) In the bottom of a greased slow cooker, arrange the chicken thighs in a single layer
4) Place the artichoke hearts over the chicken and sprinkle with garlic.
5) Pour the artichoke liquid on top.
6) Set the slow cooker on "High" and cook, covered for about 4 hours.
7) Uncover the slow cooker and stir in the sun-dried tomatoes.
8) Set the slow cooker on "High" and cook, covered for 30 minutes.
9) Serve hot with the garnishing of parsley.

 # Persian Inspired Pulled Chicken

 Servings: 4 **Cooking Time: 6 hours 5 minutes** **Preparation Time: 10 minutes**

Nutrition Information:

Calories per serving: 387; Carbohydrates: 6.7g;
Protein: 51g; Fat: 16.4g; Sugar: 2.7g; Sodium:
225mg; Fiber: 1.7g

Ingredients:	Instructions:

Ingredients:

- 1½ C. low-sodium chicken broth
- 3 tbsp. tomato paste
- 1 tbsp. ground turmeric
- 1 tsp. curry powder
- 1/8 tsp. ground cinnamon
- Salt and freshly ground black pepper, to taste
- 1 tbsp. olive oil
- 1 medium onion, chopped
- 1½ lb. boneless, skinless chicken breasts

Instructions:

1) In a bowl, add the broth, tomato paste, turmeric, curry powder, cinnamon, salt and black pepper and beat until well combined. Set aside.
2) In a skillet, heat the oil over medium-high heat and sauté the onion for about 5 minutes.
3) Transfer the cooked onion into a slow cooker and place the chicken breasts on top in a single layer.
4) Pour the broth mixture on top.
5) Set the slow cooker on "Low" and cook, covered for about 6 hours.
6) Uncover and with 2 forks, shred the chicken breasts.
7) Serve hot.

Greek Chicken Kokkinisto

 Servings: 6   **Cooking Time: 6 hours**   **Preparation Time: 15 minutes**

Nutrition Information:

Calories per serving: 448; Carbohydrates: 7.4g; Protein: 44.8g; Fat: 19.8g; Sugar: 3.7g; Sodium: 70mg; Fiber: 1.4g

Ingredients:

- 2 lb. chicken breasts, cut into 1-inch chunks
- 2 large tomatoes, grated
- 1 onion, minced
- 1 garlic clove, minced
- 2 C. white wine
- ¼ C. extra-virgin olive oil
- 2 tbsp. tomato paste
- 2 allspice berries
- 1 cinnamon stick
- 2 whole cloves
- Salt and freshly ground black pepper, to taste

Instructions:

1) In a slow cooker, place all the ingredients and stir to combine.
2) Set the slow cooker on "High" and cook, covered for about 6 hours.
3) Serve hot.

No-Fuss Chicken Orzo

 **Servings: 4** **Cooking Time: 3 hours** **Preparation Time: 15 minutes**

Nutrition Information:

Calories per serving: 652; Carbohydrates: 28.4g; Protein: 59.3g; Fat: 31.9g; Sugar: 2.9g; Sodium: 492mg; Fiber: 1.9g

Ingredients:	Instructions:

Ingredients:

- 4 boneless, skinless chicken breasts
- 3 tsp. Italian seasoning, divided
- Salt and freshly ground black pepper, to taste
- 1 tbsp. olive oil
- 1 C. fresh mushrooms, sliced
- 1 medium white onion, chopped finely
- 2 tsp. garlic, minced
- 4 tbsp. butter, melted
- 3 C. low sodium chicken broth
- 1½ C. orzo pasta
- ½ C. Parmesan cheese, shredded

Instructions:

1) Season the chicken breasts with little Italian seasonings, salt and black pepper evenly.
2) In a large non-stick skillet, heat the oil over medium-high heat and cook the chicken breasts for about 5 minutes, flipping once halfway through.
3) Transfer the chicken breasts into a greased slow cooker.
4) Top with mushrooms, onions, garlic, butter, broth, salt and black pepper.
5) Set the slow cooker on "High" and cook, covered for about 1-2 hours.
6) Remove the lid and stir in the orzo.
7) Set the slow cooker on "High" and cook, covered for about 30-45 minutes.
8) Remove the lid and with a slotted spoon transfer the chicken breasts into a bowl.
9) With 2 forks, shred the chicken meat.
10) Return the shredded chicken into the slow cooker and stir to combine.
11) Sprinkle the top with the Parmesan cheese evenly.
12) Set the slow cooker on "High" and cook, covered for about 5-10 minutes.
13) Serve hot.

# Vibrant Flavored Chicken Orzo

 Servings: 4 **Cooking Time: 2 ½ hours** **Preparation Time: 15 minutes**

Nutrition Information:

Calories per serving: 376; Carbohydrates: 30.2g; Protein: 38.3g; Fat: 10.4g; Sugar: 4.7g; Sodium: 58mg; Fiber: 2.9g

Ingredients:	Instructions:

Ingredients:

- 1 lb. boneless, skinless chicken breasts, trimmed
- 2 medium tomatoes, chopped
- 1 medium onion, halved and sliced
- 1 tsp. lemon zest, grated
- 1 tsp. Herbes de Provence
- Salt and freshly ground black pepper, to taste
- 1 C. low-sodium chicken broth
- 2 tbsp. fresh lemon juice
- ¾ C. whole-wheat orzo
- 1/3 C. black olives, pitted and quartered
- 2 tbsp. fresh parsley, chopped

Instructions:

1) Cut each chicken breast half into 4 pieces.
2) In a slow cooker, place the chicken, tomatoes, onion, lemon zest, herbs de Provence, black pepper, broth and lemon juice and stir to combine.
3) Set the slow cooker on "High" and cook, covered for about 2 hours.
4) Remove the lid and stir in the orzo.
5) Set the slow cooker on "High" and cook, covered for about 30 minutes.
6) Serve warm with the garnishing of parsley.

 # Holiday Special Turkey Breast

 Servings: 6   **Cooking Time: 6 hours 3 minutes**   **Preparation Time: 15 minutes**

Nutrition Information:

Calories per serving: 317; Carbohydrates: 16.8g;
Protein: 39.6g; Fat: 9.8g; Sugar: 12g; Sodium:
1600mg; Fiber: 3.1g

Ingredients:

- 3 tbsp. unsalted butter, softened
- 1 tbsp. orange zest, grated
- 1 tbsp. fresh thyme, chopped
- 2 tsp. fresh sage, chopped
- 2 tsp. fresh rosemary, chopped
- 1 tsp. smoked paprika
- 1 tsp. garlic powder
- 2½-3 lb. skin-on turkey breast
- Salt and freshly ground black pepper, to taste
- 2 small onions, quartered
- 1 blood orange, cut into thin rounds

Instructions:

1) In a small bowl, mix together the butter, orange zest, fresh herbs, paprika, garlic powder.
2) With your fingers, separate the turkey skin from the meat.
3) With your hands, rub half of the butter mixture under the skin.
4) Then, rub the top of the skin with remaining butter
5) Season turkey breast with salt and black pepper evenly.
6) In a slow cooker, place the onions and arrange the turkey breast on top.
7) Set the slow cooker on "Low" and cook, covered for about 5½-6 hours.
8) Meanwhile, preheat the oven to broiler.
9) Remove the turkey breast from the slow cooker and place onto a baking sheet.
10) Broil for about 3 minutes.
11) Remove from the oven and place the turkey breast onto a cutting board for about 15 minutes before slicing.
12) Cut the turkey into thin slices and serve and garnish with blood orange rounds.

 # Carnivore Diet Turkey Breast

 Servings: 8   **Cooking Time: 7 ½ hours**   **Preparation Time: 10 minutes**

Nutrition Information:

Calories per serving: 259; Carbohydrates: 6.2g;
Protein: 57.4g; Fat: 2.1g; Sugar: 1.7g; Sodium:
73mg; Fiber: 1.1g

Ingredients:

- 1 (4 lb.) boneless turkey breast, trimmed
- ½ C. chicken broth, divided
- 2 tbsp. fresh lemon juice
- 2 C. onion, chopped
- ½ C. oil-packed sun-dried tomatoes, sliced thinly
- ½ C. kalamata olives, pitted
- 1 tsp. Greek seasoning
- Salt and freshly ground black pepper, to taste
- 3 tbsp. all-purpose flour

Instructions:

1) In a slow cooker, place the turkey breast, ¼ C. of broth, lemon juice, onion, sun-dried tomatoes, olives, Greek seasoning, salt and pepper.
2) Set the slow cooker on "Low" and cook, covered for about 7 hours.
3) Meanwhile, in a bowl, add the remaining broth and flour and neat until smooth.
4) Uncover the slow cooker and stir in the flour mixture.
5) Set the slow cooker on "Low" and cook, covered for about 30 minutes.
6) Serve hot.

Gluten-Free Meatballs

 Servings: 4   **Cooking Time: 6 hours 2 minutes**   **Preparation Time: 20 minutes**

Nutrition Information:

Calories per serving: 436; Carbohydrates: 22.3g; Protein: 48.2g; Fat: 19.7g; Sugar: 11.7g; Sodium: 669mg; Fiber: 6.9g

Ingredients:

For Meatballs:
- 1¼ lb. ground turkey breast
- 1 egg
- ¼ C. Reggiano Parmigiano cheese, grated
- ¼ C. whole-wheat seasoned breadcrumbs
- ¼ C. fresh parsley, chopped finely
- 1 large garlic clove, minced
- Salt, to taste

For Sauce:
- 1 tsp. olive oil
- 4 garlic cloves, smashed
- 1 (28-oz.) can crushed tomatoes
- 1 bay leaf
- Salt and freshly ground black pepper, to taste
- ¼ C. fresh basil, chopped

Instructions:

1) For meatballs: in a large bowl, add all the ingredients and mix until well combined.
2) Make small equal-sized meatballs from the mixture.
3) For sauce: in a small skillet, heat the olive oil over medium heat and sauté the garlic for about 1 minute.
4) Stir in the tomatoes, bay leaf, salt and black pepper and remove from the heat.
5) In a slow cooker, place the meatballs and top with the sauce.
6) Set the slow cooker on "Low" and cook, covered for about 4-6 hours.
7) Serve hot with the garnishing of basil.

MEAT RECIPES

Dinner Party Brisket

Servings: 8 **Cooking Time: 11 hours 5 minutes** **Preparation Time: 15 minutes**

Nutrition Information:

Calories per serving: 367; Carbohydrates: 8.g;
Protein: 53.3g; Fat: 12.3g; Sugar: 1.5g; Sodium:
266mg; Fiber: 2.8g

Ingredients:

- 1 (3-lb.) fresh beef brisket, trimmed
- 3 tsp. dried Italian seasoning, crushed and divided
- 1 (14½-oz.) can diced tomatoes with basil, garlic and oregano with juice
- ½ C. olives, pitted
- 1 tsp. lemon peel, grated finely
- Salt and freshly ground black pepper, to taste
- ½ C. low-sodium beef broth
- 2 medium fennel bulbs, trimmed, cored and cut into wedges
- 2 tbsp. all-purpose flour
- ¼ C. cold water

Instructions:

1) Season the brisket with 1 tsp. of the Italian seasoning.
2) In a bowl, add the remaining Italian seasoning, tomatoes with juice, olives, lemon peel, salt, black pepper and broth and mix well.
3) In a slow cooker, place the brisket and top with fennel, followed by the tomato mixture.
4) Set the slow cooker on "Low" and cook, covered for about 10-11 hours.
5) Uncover the slow cooker and with a slotted spoon, transfer the brisket and vegetables onto a platter.
6) With a piece of foil, cover the meat to keep warm.
7) Skim off the fat from the top of cooking liquid.
8) In a small pan, add about 2 C. of the cooking liquid over medium heat.
9) In a small bowl, dissolve the flour in water.
10) In the pan of cooking liquid, add the flour mixture, stirring continuously.
11) Cook for about 2-3 minutes or until desired thickness of sauce, stirring continuously.
12) Cut the brisket into desired sized slices and serve with the topping of gravy.

Sunday Dinner Brisket

 Servings: 6   **Cooking Time: 8 hours 10 minutes**   **Preparation Time: 10 minutes**

Nutrition Information:

Calories per serving: 427; Carbohydrates: 7.7g;
Protein: 58.5g; Fat: 193.6g; Sugar: 3.7g; Sodium:
78mg; Fiber: 1.7g

Ingredients:

- 2½ lb. beef brisket, trimmed
- Salt and freshly ground black pepper, to taste
- 2 tsp. olive oil
- 2 medium onions, chopped
- 2 large garlic cloves, sliced
- 1 tbsp. Herbes de Provence
- 1 (15-oz.) can diced tomatoes, drained
- 2 tsp. Dijon mustard
- 1 C. dry red wine

Instructions:

1) Season the brisket with salt and black pepper evenly.
2) In a non-stick skillet, heat the oil over medium heat and cook the brisket for about 4-5 minutes per side.
3) Transfer the brisket into a slow cooker.
4) Add the remaining ingredients and stir to combine.
5) Set the slow cooker on "Low" and cook, covered for about 8 hours.
6) Uncover the slow cooker and with a slotted spoon, transfer the brisket onto a platter.
7) Cut the brisket into desired sized slices and serve with the topping of pan sauce.

Fall-Apart Tender Beef

 Servings: 12 **Cooking Time: 11 hours** **Preparation Time: 10 minutes**

Nutrition Information:

Calories per serving: 454; Carbohydrates: 43.4g; Protein: 48.3g; Fat: 10g; Sugar: 35.5g; Sodium: 1000mg; Fiber: 1.2g

Ingredients:	Instructions:

Ingredients:

- 4 lb. boneless beef chuck roast, trimmed
- 2 large onions, sliced into thin strips
- 4 celery stalks, sliced
- 4 garlic cloves, minced
- 1½ C. catsup
- 1 C. BBQ sauce
- ¼ C. molasses
- ¼ C. apple cider vinegar
- 2 tbsp. prepared yellow mustard
- ¼ tsp. red chili powder
- Fresh ground black pepper, to taste

Instructions:

1) In a slow cooker, place all the ingredients and stir to combine.
2) Set the slow cooker on "Low" and cook, covered for about 8-10 hours.
3) Uncover the slow cooker and with 2 forks, shred the meat.
4) Stir the meat with pan sauce.
5) Set the slow cooker on "Low" and cook, covered for about 1 hour.
6) Serve hot.

 # Deliciously Simple Beef

 Servings: 4   🕐 **Cooking Time: 10 hours**   🕐 **Preparation Time: 10 minutes**

Nutrition Information:

Calories per serving: 553; Carbohydrates: 4.6g;
Protein: 62.8g; Fat: 30.3g; Sugar: 18g; Sodium:
24mg; Fiber: 1g

Ingredients:	Instructions:

Ingredients:

- 1 large onion, sliced thinly
- ¼ C. extra-virgin olive oil
- 1 tbsp. garlic, minced
- 1 tsp. dried oregano
- Salt and freshly ground black pepper, to taste
- 2 tbsp. fresh lemon juice
- 2 lb. beef chuck roast, cut into bite-sized pieces

Instructions:

1) In a slow cooker, place all the ingredients except for beef cubes and stir to combine.
2) Add the beef cubes and stir to combine.
3) Set the slow cooker on "Low" and cook, covered for about 8-10 hours.
4) Serve hot.

Excellent Beef Meal

 **Servings: 6** **Cooking Time: 7 hours 4 minutes** **Preparation Time: 15 minutes**

Nutrition Information:

Calories per serving: 410; Carbohydrates: 0.9g; Protein: 53.1g; Fat: 14.2g; Sugar: 6.7g; Sodium: 1116mg; Fiber: 6.4g

Ingredients:	Instructions:

Ingredients:

- 1 tbsp. vegetable oil
- 2 lb. beef stew meat
- 1 (14 oz.) can artichoke hearts
- 1 onion
- 4 garlic cloves
- 1 (32-fluid oz.) container beef broth
- 1 (15-oz.) can tomato sauce
- 1 (14½-oz.) can diced tomatoes with juice
- ½ C. Kalamata olives, pitted
- 1 tsp. dried oregano
- 1 tsp. dried basil
- 1 tsp. dried parsley
- 1 bay leaf, crumbled
- ½ tsp. ground cumin

Instructions:

1) In a skillet, heat the oil over medium-high heat and cook the beef for about 2 minutes per side.
2) Transfer the beef into a slow cooker and top with artichoke hearts, followed by the onion and garlic.
3) Place the remaining ingredients on top.
4) Set the slow cooker on "Low" and cook, covered for about 7 hours.
5) Serve hot.

 # Lebanese Beef and Green Beans

 Servings: 4   **Cooking Time: 4 hours**   **Preparation Time: 15 minutes**

Nutrition Information:

Calories per serving: 353; Carbohydrates: 30.4g; Protein: 42.4g; Fat: 7.3g; Sugar: 15.5g; Sodium: 59mg; Fiber: 12.7g

Ingredients:

- 1 lb. beef stew meat, cubed
- 1 lb. fresh green beans, trimmed and cut in 2-inch pieces
- 1 medium onion, chopped
- 1 (32-oz.) can crushed tomatoes
- 1 tbsp. ground cinnamon
- Salt and freshly ground black pepper, to taste
- ¼ C. fresh parsley, chopped

Instructions:

1) In a slow cooker, place all the ingredients except for parsley and stir to combine.
2) Set the slow cooker on "High" and cook, covered for about 4 hours.
3) Serve hot with the garnishing of parsley.

# Grandma Style Meatballs

 Servings: 4   Cooking Time: 8 hours   Preparation Time: 20 minutes

Nutrition Information:

Calories per serving: 382; Carbohydrates: 30g; Protein: 41.1g; Fat: 12g; Sugar: 12.5g; Sodium: 723mg; Fiber: 9.4g

Ingredients:

For Meatballs:
- 1 lb. ground beef
- ¼ C. fresh parsley, minced
- ¼ C. plain breadcrumbs
- 1 tbsp. olive oil
- ½ tsp. ground allspice
- ½ tsp. ground cinnamon
- ½ tsp. ground cumin
- ¼ tsp. cayenne pepper
- Salt and freshly ground black pepper, to taste

For Veggie Sauce:
- 2 (14½-oz.) cans diced tomatoes
- 1 (14½-oz.) can tomato sauce
- 1 tsp. ground cumin
- 1 tsp. ground cinnamon
- ¼ tsp. cayenne pepper
- Pinch of salt and freshly ground black pepper
- 1 lb. frozen green beans
- ½ of sweet onion, chopped
- 2 garlic cloves, minced
- 2 tbsp. fresh parsley, chopped

Instructions:

1) For meatballs: in a large bowl, add all the ingredients and mix until well combined.
2) Make 1-inch sized meatballs from the mixture.
3) For sauce: in a slow cooker, place the diced tomatoes, tomato sauce and spices and stir to combine.
4) Add the green beans, onions and garlic and stir to combine.
5) Place the meatballs and gently submerge into the sauce.
6) Set the slow cooker on "Low" and cook, covered for about 8 hours.
7) Serve hot with the garnishing of parsley.

 # World's Best Lasagna

 Servings: 4   **Cooking Time: 6 hours** **Preparation Time: 15 minutes**

Nutrition Information:

Calories per serving: 782; Carbohydrates: 63.8g; Protein: 69.3g; Fat: 26.4g; Sugar: 6.5g; Sodium: 04mg; Fiber: 2.1g

Ingredients:

- 1 lb. lean ground beef
- 1 medium onion, chopped
- 1 jar pasta sauce
- 3-5 fresh basil leaves, chopped
- Salt, to taste
- 2 C. mozzarella cheese, shredded and divided
- 1 C. Parmesan cheese, shredded
- 15 oz. part-skim ricotta cheese
- 15 uncooked lasagna noodles

Instructions:

1) Heat a non-stick skillet over medium heat and cook the beef and onion for about 8-10 minutes.
2) Drain the grease from skillet.
3) In the skillet, add the pasta sauce, basil and salt and stir to combine.
4) Remove from the heat and set aside.
5) In a bowl, add 1 C. of the mozzarella, Parmesan and ricotta cheese and mix.
6) In a slow cooker, place ¼ of the beef mixture evenly and arrange 5 noodles on top, breaking them to fit in the pot.
7) Place half of the cheese mixture on top of the noodles.
8) Repeat the layer twice, ending with ¼ of the beef mixture.
9) Set the slow cooker on "Low" and cook, covered for about 4-6 hours.
10) In the last 20 minutes of cooking, sprinkle the lasagna with remaining mozzarella cheese.
11) Serve hot.

Rustic Lamb Shanks

 **Servings: 6**   **Cooking Time: 4 ¼ hours**   **Preparation Time: 15 minutes**

Nutrition Information:

Calories per serving: 710; Carbohydrates: 17.9g; Protein: 85.1g; Fat: 20.4g; Sugar: 2.8g; Sodium: 772mg; Fiber: 5.g

Ingredients:	Instructions:

Ingredients:

- 6 lamb shanks, frenched
- ¼ C. flour
- 3 tbsp. olive oil, divided
- 2 onions, sliced
- 4 garlic cloves, sliced thinly
- 1 (14-oz.) can marinated artichoke hearts
- ¾ C. Kalamata olives, pitted
- 2 tbsp. lemon rind, grated
- 1 tbsp. fresh oregano, chopped
- Salt and freshly ground black pepper, to taste
- ½ C. white wine
- 2½ C. chicken broth

Instructions:

1) In a large plastic bag, place the lamb shanks and flour.
2) Seal the bag and shake to coat.
3) In a pan, heat 2 tbsp. of the oil and sear the lamb shanks in 2 batches for about 4-5 minutes or until browned completely.
4) With a slotted spoon, transfer the shanks onto a platter.
5) In the same pan, heat the remaining oil over medium heat and sauté the onions and garlic for about 4-5 minutes.
6) Remove from the heat.
7) In a slow cooker, place the lamb shanks and onion mixture.
8) Top with the remaining ingredients and stir to combine.
9) Set the slow cooker on "High" and cook, covered for about 4 hours.
10) Serve hot.

Holiday Feast Lamb Shanks

 Servings: 4   **Cooking Time: 8 hours 5 minutes**   **Preparation Time: 15 minutes**

Nutrition Information:

Calories per serving: 696; Carbohydrates: 22.5g;
Protein: 83.5g; Fat: 28.6g; Sugar: 2.5g; Sodium:
49mg; Fiber: 4.7g

Ingredients:

- 4 lamb shanks
- Salt and freshly ground black pepper, to taste
- 1 tbsp. olive oil
- 1 lb. baby potatoes, halved
- 1 C. Kalamata olives
- 1 (3-oz.) jar sun-dried tomatoes
- 1 C. chicken broth
- 3 tbsp. fresh lemon juice
- 2½ tsp. dried oregano
- 1 tsp. dried rosemary
- 1 tsp. dried basil
- 1 tsp. onion powder

Instructions:

1) Season the lamb shanks with salt and black pepper evenly.
2) In a large heavy-bottomed skillet, heat the olive oil over medium-high heat and sear the lamb shanks for about 4-5 minutes or until browned completely.
3) Remove from the heat.
4) In a slow cooker, place the potatoes, olives, sun-dried tomatoes, salt, black place the lamb on top and sprinkle with dried herbs and onion powder.
5) Set the slow cooker on "Low" and cook, covered for about 8 hours.
6) Serve hot.

Succulent Leg of Lamb

 **Servings: 8** **Cooking Time: 4 hours 8 minutes** **Preparation Time: 15 minutes**

Nutrition Information:

Calories per serving: 450; Carbohydrates: 7.6g;
Protein: 48.8g; Fat: 21.4g; Sugar: 2.8g; Sodium:
182mg; Fiber: 1.7g

Ingredients:

- 1 (3-lb.) boneless leg of lamb, trimmed
- Salt and freshly ground black pepper, to taste
- 5 tbsp. extra-virgin olive oil, divided
- 6 garlic cloves, sliced thinly
- 2 tbsp. fresh lemon juice
- 6 garlic cloves, minced
- 2 tsp. fresh thyme
- 2 tsp. dried rosemary
- 1 tsp. dried oregano
- ¾ tsp. sweet paprika
- 1 lb. pearl onions, peeled
- 1 C. dry red wine
- ½ C. low-sodium beef broth

Instructions:

1) Season the leg of lamb with salt and black pepper generously.
2) Set aside at room temperature for up to 1 hour.
3) In a large skillet, heat 2 tbsp. of the oil over medium heat and sear the lamb for about 7-8 minutes or until browned completely.
4) Remove from the heat and set aside to cool slightly.
5) With a sharp knife, cut slits into the lamb on both sides.
6) Insert 1 garlic slice in each slit.
7) In a small bowl, add the remaining oil, lemon juice, minced garlic, herbs and paprika and mix well.
8) Coat the leg of lamb with oil mixture evenly.
9) In a slow cooker, place the pearl onions, wine and broth.
10) Arrange the leg of lamb on top.
11) Set the slow cooker on "High" and cook, covered for about 3-4 hours.
12) Uncover the slow cooker and with 2 tongs, transfer the leg of lamb onto a serving platter.
13) Top with pan juices and serve.

►► Melt-in-Mouth Lamb Shoulder

 **Servings: 8** **Cooking Time: 5 hours 10 minutes** **Preparation Time: 10 minutes**

Nutrition Information:

Calories per serving: 413; Carbohydrates: 3.4g; Protein: 52.3g; Fat: 19.9g; Sugar: 1.2g; Sodium: 85mg; Fiber: 0.8g

Ingredients:

- 3¼ lb. bone-in lamb shoulder, trimmed
- 2 brown onions, sliced thinly
- 5-6 garlic cloves
- ¼ C. beef broth
- ¼ C. olive oil
- 1 tbsp. dried thyme
- Salt and freshly ground black pepper, to taste

Instructions:

1) Heat a large cast-iron skillet over medium-high heat and sear the lamb shoulder for about 4-5 minutes per side.
2) Remove from the heat.
3) In a slow cooker, place the onion slices and garlic evenly and arrange the lamb shoulder on top.
4) Place the remaining ingredients on top.
5) Set the slow cooker on "High" and cook, covered for about 4-5 hours.
6) Uncover the slow cooker and with a slotted spoon, transfer the lamb shoulder onto a platter.
7) Cut the lamb shoulder into desired sized slices and serve with the topping of pan sauce.

Tangy Lamb Loin

 **Servings: 8**   **Cooking Time: 6 hours 5 minutes**   **Preparation Time: 15 minutes**

Nutrition Information:

Calories per serving: 418; Carbohydrates: 19.3g; Protein: 40.4g; Fat: 17.9g; Sugar: 1.8g; Sodium: 118mg; Fiber: 2.8g

Ingredients:

- 2 lb. lamb loin, rolled
- 6 garlic cloves, sliced thinly
- 1 bunch fresh rosemary
- 3 tbsp. olive oil
- 2¼ lb. potatoes, peeled and cubed
- ½ C. dry white wine
- ½ C. fresh lemon juice

Instructions:

1) With a sharp knife, cut slits into the lamb on both sides.
2) Insert 1 garlic slice in each slit.
3) In a large skillet, heat the oil over medium-high heat and sear the lamb loin for about 4-5 minutes or until browned from all sides.
4) Remove from the heat and insert the rosemary into the slits with garlic.
5) In the bottom of a slow cooker, place the potatoes, followed by 2 rosemary stalks and lamb loin.
6) Place the wine and lemon juice on top.
7) Set the slow cooker on "Low" and cook, covered for about 6 hours.
8) Uncover the slow cooker and with a slotted spoon, transfer the lamb loin onto a platter.
9) Cut the lamb loin into desired sized slices and serve alongside the potatoes.

Spiced Moroccan Lamb Chops

 **Servings: 4** **Cooking Time: 4 hours** **Preparation Time: 10 minutes**

Nutrition Information:

Calories per serving: 345; Carbohydrates: 0.6g;
Protein: 44.5g; Fat: 18.1g; Sugar: 0g; Sodium:
67mg; Fiber: 0.4g

Ingredients:

- 2 lb. lamb shoulder chops
- 2 tbsp. Moroccan spice rub
- ¼ lb. carrots, chopped
- ¼ C. onion, sliced
- ¼ C. fresh mint, chopped
- ¼ C. low-sodium chicken broth

Instructions:

1) Rub the lamb chops with spice rub generously.
2) In a slow cooker, place all the ingredients and stir to combine.
3) Set the slow cooker on "High" and cook, covered for about 3-4 hours.
4) Serve hot.

 # Chilly Spring Night Chops

 Servings: 4   **Cooking Time: 6 hours 5 minutes**   **Preparation Time: 15 minutes**

Nutrition Information:

Calories per serving: 600; Carbohydrates: 18.6g;
Protein: 48.9g; Fat: 33.4g; Sugar: 4.9g; Sodium:
375mg; Fiber: 6.9g

Ingredients:	Instructions:

Ingredients:

- 1 C. dry white wine
- ¼ C. butter, melted
- 2 tbsp. tomato paste
- 2 lb. lamb shoulder-blade chops
- 1 tbsp. fresh thyme, chopped
- Salt and freshly ground black pepper, to taste
- 1 tbsp. extra-virgin olive oil
- 1 large onion, sliced thinly
- 2 (6-oz.) jars marinated artichokes, drained
- ½ C. peas

Instructions:

1) In a bowl, add the wine, butter and tomato paste and beat until well combined. Set aside.
2) Rub the chops with thyme, salt and black pepper evenly.
3) In a non-stick skillet, heat the oil over medium-high heat and sear the chops for about 4-5 minutes or until browned completely.
4) Remove from the heat and place the chops in a slow cooker.
5) Place onion slices over chops and top with wine mixture, followed by the, artichokes.
6) Set the slow cooker on "Low" and cook, covered for about 6 hours.
7) In the last 30 minutes of cooking, stir in the peas.
8) Serve hot.

Favorite Lamb Pitas

 Servings: 4   **Cooking Time: 4 hours**   **Preparation Time: 20 minutes**

Nutrition Information:

Calories per serving: 439; Carbohydrates: 34.2g;
Protein: 55.7g; Fat: 42.1g; Sugar: 3.8g; Sodium:
11mg; Fiber: 1.9g

Ingredients:

For Meatballs:
- 1 lb. ground lamb
- ¾ C. fresh breadcrumbs
- 1 large egg, beaten lightly
- ¼ C. onion, chopped finely
- 1 tsp. dried mint leaves
- 1 tsp. dried oregano
- Salt and freshly ground black pepper, to taste
- ¾ C. chicken broth

For Yogurt Sauce:
- ¼ C. plain Greek yogurt
- ¼ C. cucumber, seeded and chopped finely
- 1 tsp. dried mint leaves

For Serving:
- 2 pita breads, halved
- 4 tbsp. feta cheese, crumbled

Instructions:

1) For meatballs: in a large bowl, add all the ingredients except for broth and mix until well combined.
2) Make 16 equal-sized meatballs from the mixture.
3) In a slow cooker, place the meatballs and top with the broth.
4) Set the slow cooker on "Low" and cook, covered for about 4 hours.
5) Uncover the slow cooker and drain the cooked meatballs.
6) Meanwhile, for yogurt sauce: in a bowl, add all the ingredients and mix well.
7) Arrange the pita halves onto the serving plates.
8) Place about 4 meatballs into each pita half and top with 2 tbsp. of yogurt sauce and 1 tbsp. of the feta cheese.
9) Serve immediately.

►► Greek Spiced Pork Souvlaki

Servings: 5   **Cooking Time: 8 hours**   **Preparation Time: 10 minutes**

Nutrition Information:

Calories per serving: 359; Carbohydrates: 2.2g;
Protein: 55.7g; Fat: 16.7g; Sugar: 0.7g; Sodium:
138mg; Fiber: 0.7g

Ingredients:

- ¼ C. olive oil
- ¼ C. fresh lemon juice
- 2 tbsp. red wine vinegar
- 1 tbsp. dried oregano
- 1 tbsp. dried mint
- 1 tbsp. za'atar
- 1 tbsp. garlic powder
- 1 tsp. chili flakes
- Salt, to taste
- 2 lb. boneless pork shoulder, cubed

Instructions:

1) In a medium bowl, add all the ingredients except for pork shoulder and mix well.
2) In the bottom of a slow cooker, place the pork shoulder and top with oil mixture.
3) Set the slow cooker on "Low" and cook, covered for about 8 hours.
4) Uncover the slow cooker and with 2 forks, shred the meat.
5) With a spoon, mix the meat with pan juices and serve.

# Lovely Smelling Pork Loin

 Servings: 8   **Cooking Time: 8 hours**   **Preparation Time: 10 minutes**

Nutrition Information:

Calories per serving: 242; Carbohydrates: 1.2g;
Protein: 37.8g; Fat: 8.8g; Sugar: 0.3g; Sodium:
3mg; Fiber: 0.5g

Ingredients:	Instructions:

Ingredients:

- 2 tbsp. olive oil
- ¾ C. chicken broth
- ½ tbsp. paprika
- ½ tbsp. garlic powder
- 2¼ tsp. dried sage
- 1 tsp. dried basil
- 1 tsp. dried oregano
- ¼ tsp. dried marjoram
- ¼ tsp. dried rosemary
- ¼ tsp. dried thyme
- 2½ lb. boneless pork loin, trimmed

Instructions:

1) In a medium bowl, add all the ingredients except for pork loin and mix well.
2) In the bottom of a slow cooker, place the pork loin and top with oil mixture.
3) Set the slow cooker on "Low" and cook, covered for about 7-8 hours.
4) Uncover the slow cooker and with 2 forks, shred the meat.
5) With a spoon, mix the meat with pan juices and serve.

Elegant Pork Loin

 Servings: 8 **Cooking Time: 6 hours 5 minutes** **Preparation Time: 15 minutes**

Nutrition Information:

Calories per serving: 295; Carbohydrates: 10.5g;
Protein: 46.2g; Fat: 6.7g; Sugar: 2.7g; Sodium:
283mg; Fiber: 2.6g

Ingredients:	Instructions:

Ingredients:

- 1 (3-lb.) boneless pork loin roast, trimmed
- 4 tsp. Greek seasoning
- 2 fennel bulbs, trimmed and sliced
- 4 plum tomatoes, chopped
- 1/3 C. plus 2 tbsp. low-sodium chicken broth, divided
- Salt and freshly ground black pepper, to taste
- 2 tbsp. cornstarch
- 1½ tsp. Worcestershire sauce
- ¼ C. black olives, pitted and chopped

Instructions:

1) Rub the pork loin with 1 tsp. of the Greek seasoning evenly.
2) In the bottom of a slow cooker, place the fennel slices and top with pork loin.
3) Arrange the tomatoes around the pork.
4) Top with 1/3 C. of the broth, followed by remaining Greek seasoning, salt and black pepper.
5) Set the slow cooker on "Low" and cook, covered for about 6 hours.
6) Meanwhile, in a small bowl, dissolve the cornstarch in remaining broth and Worcestershire sauce.
7) Uncover the slow cooker and with a slotted spoon, transfer the pork onto a platter.
8) With a piece, cover the pork to keep warm.
9) Through a strainer, strain the cooking liquid into a small pan.
10) Place the pan over medium-high heat and bring to a boil.
11) Add the cornstarch mixture, beating continuously until well combined.
12) Cook for about 1 minute, stirring continuously.
13) Remove from the heat and pour the sauce over pork.
14) Garnish with olives and serve.

Zero-Fussing Pork Meal

 **Servings: 4** **Cooking Time: 6 hours** **Preparation Time: 20 minutes**

Nutrition Information:

Calories per serving: 533; Carbohydrates: 35.3g;
Protein: 35.1g; Fat: 29.7g; Sugar: 8.4g; Sodium:
51mg; Fiber: 9.3g

Ingredients:

- 1 lb. lean pork, cut into bite-sized cubes
- 2 potatoes, peeled and quartered
- 1 lb. fresh green beans
- 2 carrots, peeled and sliced thinly
- 2 celery stalks, sliced thinly
- 1 large onion, chopped
- 3 fresh tomatoes, grated
- ½ C. extra-virgin olive oil
- 1 tsp. dried thyme
- Salt and freshly ground black pepper, to taste

Instructions:

1) In a slow cooker, place all the ingredients and stir to combine.
2) Set the slow cooker on "High" and cook, covered for about 6 hours.
3) Serve hot.

SEAFOOD RECIPES

Italian Flavored Salmon

 Servings: 6   **Cooking Time: 2 hours 8 minutes**   **Preparation Time: 15 minutes**

Nutrition Information:

Calories per serving: 265; Carbohydrates: 1.8g; Protein: 30.2g; Fat: 14.6g; Sugar: 0.4g; Sodium: 115mg; Fiber: 0.3g

Ingredients:

For Salmon:
- 1 tsp. Italian seasoning
- 1 tsp. garlic powder
- ½ tsp. red chili powder
- ½ tsp. sweet paprika
- Salt and freshly ground black pepper, to taste
- 2 lb. skin-on salmon fillet
- Olive oil cooking spray
- 1 lemon, cut into slices
- 1 C. low-sodium vegetable broth
- 2 tbsp. fresh lemon juice

For Lemon Sauce:
- 2/3 C. heavy cream
- ¼ C. white wine
- 3 tbsp. fresh lemon juice
- 1/8 tsp. lemon zest, grated finely
- 2-3 tbsp. fresh parsley, chopped

Instructions:

1) Line a slow cooker with a large piece of parchment paper.
2) In a small bowl, mix together the spices.
3) Spray the salmon fillet with cooking spray and rub with cooking spray evenly.
4) In the center of the prepared slow cooker, arrange the lemon slices.
5) Now, place the salmon fillet on top of lemon slices and
6) Pour the broth and lemon juice around the fish.
7) Set the slow cooker on "Low" and cook, covered for about 2 hours.
8) Meanwhile, preheat the oven to 400 degrees F.
9) Uncover the slow cooker and transfer the salmon with liquid into a baking dish.
10) Bake for about 5-8 minutes.
11) Meanwhile, for sauce: in a small pan, add the cream, wine and lemon juice over medium-high heat and bring to a boil, stirring frequently.
12) Reduce the heat to low and simmer, covered for about 8 minutes.
13) Uncover the pan and stir in the lemon zest.
14) Increase the heat to high and cook for about 2 minutes.
15) Remove from heat and set aside.
16) Remove from the oven and place the salmon fillet onto a cutting board.
17) Cut the salmon into 4 equal-sized fillets and top with sauce.
18) Garnish with parsley and serve.

Marvelous Salmon

 **Servings: 4** **Cooking Time: 2 ½ hours** **Preparation Time: 15 minutes**

Nutrition Information:

Calories per serving: 184; Carbohydrates: 0.7g;
Protein: 22.2g; Fat: 10.5g; Sugar: 0.1g; Sodium:
90mg; Fiber: 0.1g

Ingredients:

- ¾ C. fresh cilantro leaves, chopped
- 2 garlic cloves, chopped finely
- 2-3 tbsp. fresh lime juice
- 1 tbsp. olive oil
- Salt, to taste
- 1 lb. salmon fillets

Instructions:

1) In a medium bowl, add all the ingredients except for salmon fillets and mix well.
2) In the bottom of a greased slow cooker, place the salmon fillets and top with garlic mixture.
3) Set the slow cooker on "Low" and cook, covered for about 2-2½ hours.
4) With a spoon, mix the meat with pan juices and serve.

 # Nutrient-Packed Salmon

Servings: 4 **Cooking Time: 6 hours** **Preparation Time: 15 minutes**

Nutrition Information:

Calories per serving: 224; Carbohydrates: 7.9g;
Protein: 23.5g; Fat: 11.8g; Sugar: 4.1g; Sodium:
8mg; Fiber: 4.1g

Ingredients:

- 1 tbsp. Italian seasoning
- 1 tsp. onion powder
- 1 tsp. garlic powder
- Salt and freshly ground black pepper, to taste
- 1 lb. salmon fillets
- 1 tbsp. olive oil
- 1 zucchini, quartered and sliced
- 1 red bell pepper, seeded and julienned
- 1 tomato, chopped
- ½ of onion, sliced
- 3 garlic cloves, sliced

Instructions:

1) Generously, grease an oval as Pyrex dish that will fit inside the slow cooker insert.
2) In a small bowl, mix together Italian seasoning and spices.
3) Season the salmon fillets with half of the spice mixture evenly and then coat with half of the oil.
4) In a large bowl, add the vegetables, remaining spice mixture and oil and toss to coat well.
5) Place the salmon fillets into the prepared baking dish and top with vegetables.
6) With a piece of foil, cover the baking dish and place in the slow cooker.
7) Set the slow cooker on "Low" and cook, covered for about 6 hours.
8) Serve hot.

Highly Nutritious Meal

 Servings: 6 **Cooking Time: 5 hours 55 minutes** **Preparation Time: 20 minutes**

Nutrition Information:

Calories per serving: 407; Carbohydrates: 28g;
Protein: 38.4g; Fat: 15.2g; Sugar: 10.9g; Sodium:
191mg; Fiber: 9.5g

Ingredients:

- ¾ C. French lentils
- ½ C. carrots, peeled and chopped finely
- ¼ C. celery, chopped finely
- ¼ C. red onion, chopped finely
- 1 bay leaf
- 2¼ C. low-sodium chicken broth
- 1 lb. small golden beets, scrubbed and trimmed
- 1 tbsp. olive oil
- Salt and freshly ground black pepper, to taste
- 1 tbsp. raw honey
- 3-4 tbsp. fresh orange juice
- 1 tbsp. orange zest, grated
- 2 tbsp. fresh lemon juice, divided
- 1 tsp. lemon zest, grated
- 6 (5-oz.) wild salmon fillets
- 2 tbsp. fresh parsley, chopped

Instructions:

1) In a slow cooker, add the lentils, carrots, celery, onion, bay leaf and broth and mix well.
2) Arrange a piece of foil onto a smooth surface.
3) In a bowl, add the beets, oil, salt and black pepper and toss to coat well.
4) Place the beets in the center of foil and wrap tightly.
5) Arrange the foil packet on top of lentil mixture.
6) Set the slow cooker on "Low" and cook, covered for about 5-5½ hours.
7) Meanwhile, for glaze: in a small pan set, add the honey, juices and zest over medium heat and bring to a boil.
8) Reduce the heat to medium and simmer for about 1-2 minutes, stirring continuously.
9) Uncover the slow cooker and transfer the beets packet onto a plate.
10) Unwrap the foil and set the beets aside to cool slightly.
11) Peel the beets and cut into wedges.
12) Place 1 parchment paper over lentil mixture in slow cooker.
13) Season salmon fillets with salt and black pepper and brush the tops with glaze.
14) Arrange the salmon fillets over the parchment, skin side down.
15) Set the slow cooker on "Low" and cook, covered for about 25 minutes.
16) Uncover the slow cooker and transfer the salmon fillets onto a platter.
17) Discard the bay leaf and str the parsley, salt and black pepper into lentil mixture.
18) Serve lentils with salmon fillets and beet slices and serve.

Super-Healthy Dinner

Servings: 4 **Cooking Time: 1 hour 15 minutes** **Preparation Time: 15 minutes**

Nutrition Information:

Calories per serving: 507; Carbohydrates: 45.9g; Protein: 48.7g; Fat: 15.2g; Sugar: 6g; Sodium: 99mg; Fiber: 6g

Ingredients:

- 2 lb. boneless cod fillets
- Salt, to taste
- 2 (14-oz.) cans diced tomatoes
- ½ C. Kalamata olives, pitted and sliced
- ¼ C. capers
- ½ of onion, sliced
- 6 garlic cloves, sliced
- 3 tbsp. fresh parsley, chopped roughly and divided
- 1 tsp. red pepper flakes, crushed
- Freshly ground black pepper, to taste
- 3 tbsp. olive oil, divided
- 1 lemon, sliced
- 1 C. couscous
- 1 C. hot boiling water

Instructions:

1) Season each cod fillet with salt and set aside at room temperature for about 10-15 minutes.
2) In a slow cooker, place the tomato, olives, capers, onion, garlic, 1 tbsp. of parsley, red pepper flakes, black pepper and 1½ tbsp. of olive oil and mix well.
3) Place the cod fillets over the sauce in a single layer and spoon some of the tomato mixture on top.
4) Arrange 2 lemon slices on top.
5) Set the slow cooker on "High" and cook, covered for about 1 hour.
6) Uncover the slow cooker and with a slotted spoon, transfer the cod fillets onto a platter.
7) Place about 2/3 of the sauce on top of cod fillets.
8) In the slow cooker with remaining sauce, add the couscous, boiling water and a little salt and mix well.
9) Set the slow cooker on "High" and cook, covered for about 10 minutes.
10) Uncover the slow cooker and with a fork fluff the couscous.
11) Stir in the remaining olive oil and serve with cod fillets.

Paleo-Friendly Tilapia

 **Servings: 4** **Cooking Time: 2 hours** **Preparation Time: 15 minutes**

Nutrition Information:

Calories per serving: 132; Carbohydrates: 8.5g;
Protein: 22.8g; Fat: 1.4g; Sugar: 5.1g; Sodium:
92mg; Fiber: 2.2g

Ingredients:

- 1 (15-oz.) can diced tomatoes
- 1 bell pepper, seeded and chopped
- 1 small onion, chopped
- 1 garlic cloves, minced
- 1 tsp. dried rosemary
- 1/3 C. low-sodium chicken broth
- Salt and freshly ground black pepper, to taste
- 1 lb. tilapia fillets

Instructions:

1) In a slow cooker, place all the ingredients except for tilapia and stir to combine.
2) Place the tilapia on top and gently submerge in sauce.
3) Set the slow cooker on "High" and cook, covered for about 2 hours.
4) Serve hot.

Winner Halibut

  Servings: 2 **Cooking Time: 2 hours** **Preparation Time: 10 minutes**

Nutrition Information:

Calories per serving: 258; Carbohydrates: 1.7g; Protein: 36.4g; Fat: 11.2g; Sugar: 0.2g; Sodium: 74mg; Fiber: 0.4g

Ingredients:

- 12 oz. halibut fillet
- Salt and freshly ground black pepper, to taste
- 1 tbsp. fresh lemon juice
- 1 tbsp. olive oil
- 1½ tsp. dried dill

Instructions:

1) Arrange a large 18-inch piece of greased piece foil onto a smooth surface.
2) Season the halibut fillet with salt and black pepper.
3) In a small bowl, add the lemon juice, oil and dill and mix well.
4) Place the halibut fillet in the center of foil and drizzle with oil mixture.
5) Carefully bring up the edges of foil and crimp them together, leaving plenty of air inside of the foil packet.
6) Place the foil packet in the bottom of a slow cooker.
7) Set the slow cooker on "High" and cook, covered for about 1½-2 hours.
8) Uncover the slow cooker and remove the foil packet.
9) Carefully open the foil packet and serve.

Unique Salmon Risotto

 Servings: 4 Cooking Time: 1 hour 20 minutes Preparation Time: 15 minutes

Nutrition Information:

Calories per serving: 534; Carbohydrates: 53.2g; Protein: 36.1g; Fat: 17.3g; Sugar: 1.5g; Sodium: 686mg; Fiber: 2.2g

Ingredients:

- 2 tbsp. olive oil
- 2 shallots, chopped
- ½ of medium cucumber, peeled, seeded and chopped
- 1¼ C. Arborio rice
- 3 C. hot vegetable broth
- ½ C. white wine
- 1¼ lb. skinless salmon fillet, chopped
- Salt and freshly ground black pepper, to taste
- 1 scallion, chopped
- 3 tbsp. fresh dill, chopped

Instructions:

1) In a pan, heat the oil over medium-high heat and sauté the shallot and cucumber for about 2-3 minutes.
2) Reduce the heat to low and cook, covered for about 15 minutes.
3) Add the rice and stir to combine.
4) Increase the heat to high and sauté for about 1 minute.
5) Remove from the heat and transfer the rice mixture into a slow cooker.
6) Pour the hot broth and wine on top.
7) Set the slow cooker on "High" and cook, covered for about 45 minutes.
8) Uncover the slow cooker and stir in the salmon pieces, salt and black pepper.
9) Set the slow cooker on "High" and cook, covered for about 15 minutes.
10) Switch off the slow cooker and let the risotto stand, covered for about 5 minutes.
11) Uncover the slow cooker and stir in the scallion and dill.
12) Serve hot.

Delish Dinner Shrimp

Servings: 4   **Cooking Time: 5 hours**   **Preparation Time: 20 minutes**

Nutrition Information:

Calories per serving: 217 Carbohydrates: 16.9g; Protein: 28.2g; Fat: 2.8g; Sugar: 10.2g; Sodium: 05mg; Fiber: 10.2g

Ingredients:

- 1 medium onion, chopped
- ½ of medium green bell pepper, seeded and chopped
- 1 (14½-oz.) can whole tomatoes, undrained and chopped roughly
- 1 (2½-oz.) jar sliced mushrooms
- ¼ C. ripe olives, pitted and sliced
- 2 garlic cloves, minced
- 1 (14½-oz.) can low-sodium chicken broth
- 1 (8-oz.) can tomato sauce
- ½ C. dry white wine
- ½ C. orange juice
- 1 tsp. dried basil leaves
- 2 bay leaves
- ¼ tsp. fennel seed, crushed
- Salt and freshly ground black pepper, to taste
- 1 lb. medium shrimp, peeled

Instructions:

1) In a slow cooker, place all the ingredients except for shrimp and stir to combine.
2) Set the slow cooker on "Low" and cook, covered for about 4-4½ hours.
3) Uncover the slow cooker and stir in the shrimp.
4) Set the slow cooker on "Low" and cook, covered for about 20-30 minutes.
5) Uncover the slow cooker and discard the bay leaves.
6) Serve hot.

Loveable Feta Shrimp

 Servings: 6   **Cooking Time: 2 hours 25 minutes** **Preparation Time: 15 minutes**

Nutrition Information:

Calories per serving: 324; Carbohydrates: 14g; Protein: 31.3g; Fat: 15.1g; Sugar: 9.4g; Sodium: 819mg; Fiber: 4.7g

Ingredients:

- ¼ C. extra-virgin olive oil
- 1 medium onion, chopped
- 1 (28-oz.) can crushed tomatoes
- ½ C. dry white wine
- ½ tsp. dried oregano
- Pinch of red pepper flakes, crushed
- Salt, to taste
- 1½ lb. medium shrimp, peeled and deveined
- 1 C. feta cheese, crumbled
- 2 tbsp. fresh parsley, chopped

Instructions:

1) In a skillet, heat the oil over medium heat and cook the onion about 10 minutes, stirring frequently.
2) Remove from the heat and transfer the onion into a large slow cooker.
3) Add the tomatoes, wine, oregano, red pepper flakes and salt and stir to combine.
4) Set the slow cooker on "High" and cook, covered for about 2 hours.
5) Uncover the slow cooker and stir in the shrimp.
6) Sprinkle with feta cheese evenly.
7) Set the slow cooker on "High" and cook, covered for about 10-15 minutes.
8) Serve hot with the garnishing of parsley

 # Luncheon Party Meal

 Servings: 4   **Cooking Time: 4 ½ hours**   **Preparation Time: 20 minutes**

Nutrition Information:

Calories per serving: 206; Carbohydrates: 10.8g; Protein: 16.7g; Fat: 8.9g; Sugar: 5.5g; Sodium: 423mg; Fiber: 2.5g

Ingredients:

- 1 (14½-oz.) can diced tomatoes, drained
- 1 C. red sweet pepper, seeded and chopped
- 1 C. zucchini, sliced
- 2 garlic cloves, minced
- ½ C. dry white wine
- 8 oz. frozen medium shrimp, thawed
- 8 Kalamata olives, pitted and chopped roughly
- ¼ C. fresh basil, chopped
- 1 tbsp. olive oil
- 1½ tsp. fresh rosemary, chopped
- Salt, to taste
- 2 oz. feta cheese, crumbled

Instructions:

1) In a lightly greased slow cooker, place the tomatoes, sweet pepper, zucchini, garlic and wine and mix well.
2) Set the slow cooker on "Low" and cook, covered for about 4 hours.
3) Uncover the slow cooker and stir in the shrimp.
4) Set the slow cooker on "High" and cook, covered for about 30 minutes.
5) Uncover the slow cooker and stir in the remaining ingredients.
6) Serve hot with the topping of feta cheese.

Easiest Shrimp Scampi

 **Servings: 4** **Cooking Time: 1 ½ hours** **Preparation Time: 15 minutes**

Nutrition Information:

Calories per serving: 252; Carbohydrates: 2.6g; Protein: 26.4g; Fat: 14.8g; Sugar: 0.2g; Sodium: 406mg; Fiber: 0.1g

Ingredients:	Instructions:

Ingredients:

- 1 lb. raw shrimp, peeled and deveined
- ¼ C. chicken broth
- 2 tbsp. butter
- 2 tbsp. olive oil
- 1 tbsp. fresh lemon juice
- 1 tbsp. garlic, minced
- 1 tbsp. dried parsley
- Salt and freshly ground black pepper, to taste

Instructions:

1) In a slow cooker, place all the ingredients and stir to combine.
2) Set the slow cooker on "High" and cook, covered for about 1½ hours.
3) Uncover the slow cooker and stir the mixture.
4) Serve hot.

Amazingly Tasty Shrimp Orzo

 Servings: 6   **Cooking Time: 3 hours 16 minutes**   **Preparation Time: 15 minutes**

Nutrition Information:

Calories per serving: 633; Carbohydrates: 57.9g; Protein: 35.4g; Fat: 30.2g; Sugar: 8.5g; Sodium: 390mg; Fiber: 5.3g

Ingredients:	Instructions:

Ingredients:

- 2 C. uncooked orzo pasta
- 2 tsp. dried basil
- 3 tbsp. olive oil, divided
- 2 tbsp. butter
- 1½ tbsp. shallot, chopped
- 1 (14½-oz.) can diced tomatoes, drained
- 3 garlic cloves, minced
- 2 tsp. dried oregano
- 1 lb. jumbo shrimp, peeled and deveined
- 1 C. oil-packed sun-dried tomatoes, chopped
- 1½ C. Greek olives, pitted
- 2½ C. feta cheese, crumbled

Instructions:

1) In a large pan of the salted boiling water, cook the orzo for about 8-10 minutes or according to the package's directions.
2) Drain the orzo and rinse under cold running water.
3) Transfer the orzo into a large bowl with basil and 1 tbsp. of oil and toss to coat well. Set aside.
4) In a large skillet, heat the remaining oil and butter over medium heat and sauté the shallot for about 2-3 minutes.
5) Add the tomatoes, garlic and oregano and cook for about 1-2 minutes.
6) Add the shrimp and sun-dried tomatoes and cook for about 1 minute.
7) Remove from the heat and place the shrimp mixture into a greased slow cooker.
8) Add the orzo mixture, olives and cheese and stir to combine.
9) Set the slow cooker on "Low" and cook, covered for about 2-3 hours.
10) Serve hot.

Delightful Shrimp Pasta

 **Servings: 4** **Cooking Time: 7 ¼ hours** **Preparation Time: 15 minutes**

Nutrition Information:

Calories per serving: 212; Carbohydrates: 14.6g; Protein: 30.6g; Fat: 3.8g; Sugar: 7.9g; Sodium: 828mg; Fiber: 3.2g

Ingredients:

- 1 (14½-oz.) can peeled tomatoes, chopped
- 1 (6-oz.) can tomato paste
- 2 tbsp. fresh parsley, minced
- 1 garlic clove, minced
- 1 tsp. dried oregano
- 1 tsp. dried basil
- 1 tsp. seasoned salt
- 1 lb. cooked shrimp
- Salt and freshly ground black pepper, to taste
- ¼ C. parmesan cheese, shredded

Instructions:

1) In a slow cooker, place all the ingredients except for shrimp and Parmesan and stir to combine.
2) Set the slow cooker on "Low" and cook, covered for about 6-7 hours.
3) Uncover the slow cooker and stir in the cooked shrimp.
4) Sprinkle with parmesan cheese.
5) Set the slow cooker on "High" and cook, covered for about 15 minutes.
6) Serve hot.

Meltingly Tender Octopus

 **Servings: 4** **Cooking Time: 6 hours** **Preparation Time: 20 minutes**

Nutrition Information:

Calories per serving: 308; Carbohydrates: 18.5g;
Protein: 30.6g; Fat: 12.3g; Sugar: 1.6g; Sodium:
30mg; Fiber: 3.3g

Ingredients:

- 1½ lb. octopus
- 6 fingerlings potatoes
- ½ lemon, cut into slices
- Salt and freshly ground black pepper, to taste
- Water, as required
- 3 tbsp. extra-virgin olive oil
- 3 tbsp. capers

Instructions:

1) Remove the beak, eyes and any other parts of octopus.
2) Rinse the inside and outside of the octopus head and tentacles.
3) Cut off the head of the octopus at its base.
4) In a pan of the boiling water, dip the octopus with a pair of for about 10-15 seconds.
5) Now, place the octopus in a slow cooker.
6) Place the potatoes, lemon slices, salt, black pepper and enough water to cover.
7) Set the slow cooker on "High" and cook, covered for about 5-6 hours.
8) Uncover the slow cooker and drain the octopus in a colander.
9) With a slotted spoon, transfer the potatoes onto a platter.
10) With paper towels, pat dry the potatoes and cut into thin slices.
11) Cut the octopus into thin slices.
12) In a large bowl, add the octopus, potatoes, oil, capers, salt and black pepper and toss to coat.
13) Serve immediately.

SOUP & STEW RECIPES

59

Healthy Chicken Soup

 Servings: 6   **Cooking Time: 4 hours**   **Preparation Time: 15 minutes**

Nutrition Information:

Calories per serving: 377; Carbohydrates: 36.8g; Protein: 47.2g; Fat: 4.2g; Sugar: 2.5g; Sodium: 95mg; Fiber: 11.7g

Ingredients:

- 1½ lb. cooked rotisserie chicken, shredded
- 2 (15-oz.) cans Great Northern beans, drained and rinsed
- 3 carrots, peeled and chopped
- 3 celery stalks, chopped
- 4 C. fresh baby spinach
- 1 yellow onion, chopped
- 3 garlic cloves, minced
- 2 bay leaves
- Salt and freshly ground black pepper, to taste
- 4 C. low-sodium chicken broth
- 2 C. water

Instructions:

1) In a slow cooker, place all the ingredients and stir to combine.
2) Set the slow cooker on "High" and cook, covered for about 3-4 hours.
3) Serve hot.

Warming Chicken Soup

 **Servings: 4** **Cooking Time: 7 hours 10 hours** **Preparation Time: 15 minutes**

Nutrition Information:

Calories per serving: 501; Carbohydrates: 40.5g; Protein: 51.2g; Fat: 13.6g; Sugar: 6.9g; Sodium: 1200mg; Fiber: 5.5g

Ingredients:	Instructions:

Ingredients:

- 3 boneless, skinless chicken breasts, cut into ½-inch cubes
- 1 onion, chopped
- 3 carrots, peeled and chopped
- 3 celery stalks, chopped
- 3 garlic cloves, minced
- 1 bay leaf
- 5½ C. chicken broth
- Salt and freshly ground black pepper, to taste
- 2½ C. egg noodles
- 1 C. frozen peas
- ¼ C. fresh parsley, chopped

Instructions:

1) In a slow cooker, place all the ingredients except for noodles, peas and parsley and stir to combine.
2) Set the slow cooker on "Low" and cook, covered for about 6 hours.
3) Uncover the slow cooker and stir in the egg noodles and peas.
4) Set the slow cooker on "High" and cook, covered for about 7-10 minutes.
5) Uncover the slow cooker and stir in the parsley.
6) Serve immediately.

 # Unbelievably Delicious Chicken Soup

 Servings: 8   **Cooking Time: 6 hours 20 minutes**   **Preparation Time: 20 minutes**

Nutrition Information:

Calories per serving: 323; Carbohydrates: 19.5g;
Protein: 31.8g; Fat: 12g; Sugar: 2.4g; Sodium:
44mg; Fiber: 1.1g

Ingredients:

- 1½ lb. chicken breasts
- ¾ C. long-grain white rice
- 2 large carrots, peeled and cut into ¼-inch slices
- 1 yellow onion, chopped
- 1 celery stalk, diced
- Salt and freshly ground black pepper, to taste
- 6 C. chicken broth
- 2 tbsp. butter, melted
- 2 tbsp. all-purpose flour
- 2 eggs
- ¼ C. fresh lemon juice
- 2-3 tbsp. feta cheese, crumbled

Instructions:

1) In a slow cooker, place the chicken breasts, rice, carrots, onion, celery, salt, black pepper and broth and stir to combine.
2) Set the slow cooker on "Low" and cook, covered for about 4-6 hours.
3) Uncover the slow cooker and with a slotted spoon, transfer the chicken breasts onto a plate.
4) In a bowl, add the butter and flour and beat until smooth.
5) Add about 1 C. of hot soup in the bowl of the flour mixture and beat until smooth.
6) Add the flour mixture into the slow cooker with remaining soup and stir to combine.
7) Add the lemon juice and stir to combine.
8) In a bowl, add the eggs and beat until frothy.
9) Add 1 tbsp. of the hot soup into the bowl of beaten eggs and beat well.
10) Repeat this process 3 times.
11) Add the egg mixture into the slow cooker with remaining soup and stir to combine.
12) With 2 forks, shred the meat of chicken breasts.
13) In the soup, add the shredded meat and stir to combine.
14) Set the slow cooker on "High" and cook, covered for about 15-20 minutes.
15) Serve hot with the topping of feta.

Best Dinner Option Soup

 Servings: 4   **Cooking Time: 4 ½ hours**   **Preparation Time: 15 minutes**

Nutrition Information:

Calories per serving: 845; Carbohydrates: 96.7g;
Protein: 63.6g; Fat: 24.9g; Sugar: 16.4g; Sodium:
2000mg; Fiber: 11g

Ingredients:	Instructions:

Ingredients:

- 12-16 frozen turkey meatballs
- 1 (14-oz.) can chickpeas, drained and rinsed
- 2 medium carrots, peeled and chopped
- 1 medium onion, chopped
- 1 (28-oz.) can fire-roasted diced tomatoes
- 1 garlic clove, minced
- 1 tbsp. lemon zest, grated
- 4 C. chicken broth
- 1 (8-oz.) can tomato sauce
- ½ tsp. dried oregano
- ½ tsp. dried parsley
- Salt and freshly ground black pepper, to taste
- 2-3 C. fresh baby spinach leaves
- 1 C. orzo

Instructions:

1) In a slow cooker, place all the ingredients except for spinach and orzo and stir to combine.
2) Set the slow cooker on "High" and cook, covered for about 3-4 hours.
3) Uncover the slow cooker and stir in the spinach and orzo.
4) Set the slow cooker on "High" and cook, covered for about 20-30 minutes.
5) Serve hot.

 # Cozy-Nights Meat Soup

 Servings: 8   **Cooking Time: 4 ½ hours**   **Preparation Time: 20 minutes**

Nutrition Information:

Calories per serving: 832; Carbohydrates: 78g;
Protein: 65.2g; Fat: 29.2g; Sugar: 11.9g; Sodium:
23mg; Fiber: 16.4g

Ingredients:	Instructions:

Ingredients:

- 1 lb. dried chickpeas, soaked for 12 hours and drained
- 2 lb. skinless chicken drumsticks
- 1 (4-oz.) piece Serrano ham, cut into ½-inch cubes
- 4 oz. Spanish chorizo, cut into ½-inch rounds
- 8 baby red potatoes, scrubbed and halved
- 2 medium carrots, peeled and cut into ½-inch chunks
- 1 large leek, (white and light green parts), halved and sliced thinly
- 2 celery stalks, chopped
- 3 large garlic cloves, minced
- 1 tbsp. fresh oregano, chopped
- 2 bay leaves
- 1 tbsp. smoked paprika
- ½ tsp. saffron threads
- Salt and freshly ground black pepper, to taste
- 6 C. hot chicken broth
- 1 lb. cabbage, cored and cut into 8 wedges
- ½ C. fresh parsley, chopped

Instructions:

1) In a slow cooker, place all the ingredients except for cabbage and parsley and stir to combine.
2) Set the slow cooker on "High" and cook, covered for about 4 hours.
3) Uncover the slow cooker and with a slotted spoon, transfer the chicken breasts onto a cutting board.
4) In the slow cooker, place the cabbage and submerge into the soup.
5) Set the slow cooker on "High" and cook, covered for about 30 minutes.
6) Meanwhile, remove the bones from chicken breasts and cut the meat into bite-sized pieces.
7) Uncover the slow cooker and discard the bay leaves.
8) Stir in the chicken pieces and serve with the garnishing of parsley.

Tuscan Dinner Soup

 **Servings: 6** **Cooking Time: 8 ¾ hours** **Preparation Time: 20 minutes**

Nutrition Information:

Calories per serving: 447; Carbohydrates: 34.1g; Protein: 29.9g; Fat: 20.5g; Sugar: 6.1g; Sodium: 1790mg; Fiber: 8.2g

Ingredients:

- 16 oz. dried Great Northern beans, rinsed and drained
- 2 C. butternut squash, peeled and chopped
- 2 carrots, peeled and chopped
- 2 celery stalks, chopped
- 1 medium yellow onion, chopped
- 4 large garlic cloves, minced
- 4 fresh thyme sprigs
- 4 bay leaves
- Salt and freshly ground black pepper, to taste
- 8 C. chicken broth
- 1 lb. ground Italian sausage
- 4 C. fresh baby kale leaves
- 3 tbsp. tomato paste
- ¼ C. Parmesan cheese, shredded

Instructions:

1) In a slow cooker, place the beans, squash, carrots, celery, onion, garlic, thyme sprigs, bay leaves, salt, black pepper and broth and stir to combine.
2) Set the slow cooker on "Low" and cook, covered for about 8 hours.
3) Meanwhile, make small sized balls from the sausage and refrigerate before cooking.
4) Uncover the slow cooker and transfer about ½ C. of the soup broth into a small bowl.
5) In the bowl of soup, add the tomato paste and beat until smooth.
6) Add the mixture into the slow cooker and stir to combine.
7) Add the kale and sausage meatballs and gently, stir to combine.
8) Set the slow cooker on "Low" and cook, covered for about 40-45 minutes.
9) Serve hot with the topping of Parmesan cheese.

Pure Comfort Soup

 Servings: 10   **Cooking Time: 8 hours 5 minutes**   **Preparation Time: 20 minutes**

Nutrition Information:

Calories per serving: 439; Carbohydrates: 33.9g;
Protein: 23.6g; Fat: 22.6g; Sugar: 14.8g; Sodium:
98mg; Fiber: 2.3g

Ingredients:

- 1 lb. ground Italian sausage
- 2 large carrots, peeled and chopped
- 2 celery stalks, chopped
- 1 onion, chopped
- 4 garlic cloves, minced
- 1 tbsp. Italian seasoning
- Salt, to taste
- 4 C. beef broth
- ¼ C. cornstarch
- ¼ C. water
- 36 oz. evaporated milk
- 12 oz. three cheese tortellini
- 5 C. fresh baby spinach
- 1 C. milk

Instructions:

1) Heat a non-stick skillet over medium heat and cook the sausage for about 8-10 minutes.
2) Drain the grease and transfer the sausage into a slow cooker.
3) Add the carrots, celery, onion, garlic, Italian seasoning, salt and broth and stir to combine.
4) Set the slow cooker on "Low" and cook, covered for about 7 hours.
5) Meanwhile, in a small bowl, dissolve the cornstarch in water.
6) Uncover the slow cooker and skim off the fat from the top of soup.
7) Add the cornstarch mixture and evaporated milk mix until well combined.
8) Add the tortellini and mix well.
9) Set the slow cooker on "High" and cook, covered for about 45 minutes.
10) Uncover the slow cooker and stir in the spinach.
11) Set the slow cooker on "High" and cook, covered for about 10 minutes.
12) Uncover the slow cooker and stir in the milk, 1/3 C. at a time.
13) Serve immediately.

 # Flavorsome Shrimp Soup

 Servings: 6 **Cooking Time: 5 hours** **Preparation Time: 15 minutes**

Nutrition Information:

Calories per serving: 234; Carbohydrates: 11.5g;
Protein: 37.1g; Fat: 3.5g; Sugar: 7.2g; Sodium:
1003mg; Fiber: 2.3g

Ingredients:

- 1 onion, chopped
- ½ of green bell pepper, seeded and chopped
- 1 (14½-oz.) can diced tomatoes with juice
- 2½ oz. canned mushrooms
- ¼ C. black olives, pitted and sliced
- 2 garlic cloves, minced
- 1 (8-oz.) can tomato sauce
- 2 bay leaves
- 1 tsp. dried basil
- ¼ tsp. fennel seed, crushed
- Salt and freshly ground black pepper, to taste
- ½ C. dry white wine
- ½ C. orange juice
- 2 (14-oz.) cans chicken broth
- 2 lb. medium shrimp, peeled and deveined

Instructions:

1) In a slow cooker, place all the ingredients except for shrimp and stir to combine.
2) Set the slow cooker on "Low" and cook, covered for about 4-4½ hours.
3) Uncover the slow cooker and stir in the shrimp.
4) Set the slow cooker on "Low" and cook, covered for about 20-30 minutes.
5) Uncover the slow cooker and discard the bay leaves.
6) Serve hot.

# Detox Vegetarian Soup

Servings: 8 **Cooking Time: 6 hours** **Preparation Time: 20 minutes**

Nutrition Information:

Calories per serving: 370; Carbohydrates: 44g; Protein: 17.9g; Fat: 14.6g; Sugar: 6.2g; Sodium: 42mg; Fiber: 15.5g

Ingredients:

- 1 C. green lentils
- ¾ C. yellow split peas
- 2 C. butternut squash, peeled and cubed
- 2 C. potatoes, chopped
- 2 C. carrots, peeled and sliced
- 2 C. celery stalks, chopped
- 1 onion, chopped
- 5 garlic cloves, minced
- 8-10 C. vegetable broth
- 2 tsp. Herbes de Provence
- Salt, to taste
- ½ C. olive oil
- 2-3 C. fresh kale, tough ribs removed and chopped
- 1 C. fresh parsley, chopped

Instructions:

1) In a slow cooker, place all the ingredients except for oil, kale and parsley and stir to combine.
2) Set the slow cooker on "High" and cook, covered for about 5-6 hours.
3) Uncover the slow cooker and transfer about 4 C. of soup in a bowl.
4) Set aside to cool for about 2-3 minutes.
5) Meanwhile, in the remaining soup, add the kale and parsley and stir until wilted.
6) In a blender, add the cooled soup and oil and pulse until slightly smooth.
7) Return the pureed soup into the slow cooker with the remaining soup and stir to combine.
8) Serve immediately.

Aromatic Veggie Soup

 Servings: 8   **Cooking Time: 4 hours**   **Preparation Time: 20 minutes**

Nutrition Information:

Calories per serving: 155; Carbohydrates: 22.6g; Protein: 5.4g; Fat: 5.8g; Sugar: 6.8g; Sodium: 282mg; Fiber: 5.4g

Ingredients:	Instructions:

Ingredients:

- 2 russet potatoes, scrubbed and cut into ¼-inch thick rounds
- 2 large carrots, peeled and sliced into rounds
- 1½ lb. green cabbage, cored and chopped
- 2 medium onions, sliced into half
- 2 garlic cloves, minced
- 1 tbsp. ground cumin
- 1 tsp. sweet Spanish paprika
- ½ tsp. ground coriander
- ¼ tsp. ground turmeric
- 1 bay leaf
- Salt and freshly ground black pepper, to taste
- 1 C. tomato sauce
- 3 tbsp. extra-virgin olive oil
- 7 C. low-sodium vegetable broth
- ½ C. fresh dill
- 2 tbsp. fresh lemon juice

Instructions:

1) In a slow cooker, place all the ingredients except for dill and lemon juice and stir to combine.
2) Set the slow cooker on "High" and cook, covered for about 4 hours.
3) Uncover the slow cooker and stir in the dill and lemon juice.
4) Serve hot.

►► Traditional Minestrone Soup

 Servings: 12 **Cooking Time: 8 ½ hours** **Preparation Time: 20 minutes**

Nutrition Information:

Calories per serving: 370; Carbohydrates: 62.4g;
Protein: 23.7g; Fat: 4.1g; Sugar: 8.8g; Sodium:
45mg; Fiber: 18.4g

Ingredients:

- 2 medium potatoes, peeled and chopped
- 2 medium carrots, peeled and chopped
- 2 celery stalks, chopped
- 1 (14½ oz.) can diced tomatoes with juice
- 1 medium onion, chopped
- 3 garlic cloves, minced
- 2 bay leaves
- 1 tbsp. Italian seasoning
- Salt and freshly ground black pepper, to taste
- 1 (32-oz.) carton vegetable broth
- 3 C. tomato juice
- 2 C. water
- 1 small zucchini, chopped
- 1 (16-oz.) can kidney beans, rinsed and drained
- 1 (15-oz.) can cannellini beans, rinsed and drained
- 1 (14½-oz.) can cut green beans, drained
- 1 C. uncooked ditalini pasta
- 1 C. Parmesan cheese, shredded

Instructions:

1) In a slow cooker, place the potatoes, carrots, celery, tomatoes with juice, onion, garlic, bay leaves, Italian seasoning, salt, black pepper, broth, tomato juice and water and stir to combine.
2) Set the slow cooker on "Low" and cook, covered for about 6-8 hours.
3) Uncover the slow cooker and stir in the remaining ingredients except for cheese.
4) Set the slow cooker on "High" and cook, covered for about 30 minutes.
5) Uncover the slow cooker and discard bay leaves.
6) Serve hot with the topping of Parmesan cheese.

Filling Vegetarian Soup

Nutrition Information:

Calories per serving: 379; Carbohydrates: 64.9g;
Protein: 25.4g; Fat: 3.1g; Sugar: 6.1g; Sodium:
779mg; Fiber: 13.4g

Ingredients:

- 3 (14 -oz.) cans vegetable broth
- 1 (15-oz.) can tomato puree
- 1 (15-oz.) can white beans, rinsed and drained
- ½ C. converted white rice
- ½ C. onion, chopped finely
- 2 garlic cloves, minced
- 1 tsp. dried basil, crushed
- Salt and freshly ground black pepper, to taste
- 8 C. fresh spinach, chopped
- ¼ C. Parmesan cheese, shredded

Instructions:

1) In a slow cooker, place all the ingredients except for spinach and cheese and stir to combine.
2) Set the slow cooker on "High" and cook, covered for about 2½-3½ hours.
3) Uncover the slow cooker and stir in the spinach until wilted.
4) Serve hot with the topping of Parmesan cheese.

 # Nutritious Vegan Soup

 Servings: 8   **Cooking Time: 8 hours**   **Preparation Time: 15 minutes**

Nutrition Information:

Calories per serving: 338; Carbohydrates: 58.5g;
Protein: 20.9g; Fat: 3.2gg; Sugar: 5g; Sodium:
28mg; Fiber: 14.6g

Ingredients:

- 1 C. uncooked quinoa, rinsed
- 1 (15-oz.) can Great Northern beans, drained and rinsed
- 2 (14½-oz.) cans petite diced tomatoes
- 1 onion, chopped
- 3 garlic cloves, minced
- ½ tsp. dried basil
- ½ tsp. dried oregano
- ¼ tsp. dried thyme
- ¼ tsp. dried rosemary
- 2 bay leaves
- Salt and freshly ground black pepper, to taste
- 6 C. vegetable broth
- 6-8 C. fresh kale, tough ribs removed and chopped

Instructions:

1) In a slow cooker, place all the ingredients except for kale and stir to combine.
2) Set the slow cooker on "Low" and cook, covered for about 7-8 hours.
3) Uncover the slow cooker and stir in the kale until wilted.
4) Serve hot.

High-Protein Lentil Soup

 Servings: 6 **Cooking Time: 8 hours 10 minutes** **Preparation Time: 15 minutes**

Nutrition Information:

Calories per serving: 474; Carbohydrates: 58.1g;
Protein: 22.8g; Fat: 17.8g; Sugar: 5g; Sodium:
67mg; Fiber: 27.7g

Ingredients:	Instructions:

Ingredients:

- 18 oz. lentils
- 3 carrots, peeled and chopped
- 1 large red onion, chopped
- 2 garlic cloves,
- 2 tbsp. tomato paste
- 2 tsp. dried oregano
- 2 bay leaves, crumbled
- Salt and freshly ground black pepper, to taste
- ½ C. olive oil
- 6-7 C. water

Instructions:

1) In a pan of the water, add the lentils and bring to a boil.
2) Cook for about 10 minutes.
3) Drain the lentils well and transfer into the slow cooker.
4) Add the remaining ingredients and stir to combine.
5) Set the slow cooker on "Low" and cook, covered for about 6-8 hours.
6) Serve hot.

Family Favorite Pasta Soup

 Servings: 6   **Cooking Time: 8 hours**   **Preparation Time: 15 minutes**

Nutrition Information:

Calories per serving: 514; Carbohydrates: 82.1g; Protein: 28g; Fat: 9g; Sugar: 5.7g; Sodium: 95mg; Fiber: 14.1g

Ingredients:

- 2 C. onions, chopped
- 1 C. celery, chopped
- 1 C. carrots, peeled and chopped
- 6 C. low-sodium chicken broth
- 4 tsp. Italian seasoning
- Salt, to taste
- 4 C. cooked whole-wheat rotini pasta
- 1 (15-oz.) can white beans, rinsed and drained
- 4 C. fresh baby spinach
- 4 tbsp. fresh basil, chopped and divided
- 2 tbsp. extra-virgin olive oil
- ½ C. Parmigiano-Reggiano cheese, grated

Instructions:

1) In a slow cooker, place the onions, celery, carrots, Italian seasoning and salt and stir to combine.
2) Set the slow cooker on "Low" and cook, covered for about 7¼ hours.
3) Uncover the slow cooker and stir in the cooked chicken, pasta, beans, spinach and 2 tbsp. of the basil.
4) Set the slow cooker on "Low" and cook, covered for about 45 minutes.
5) Transfer the soup into serving bowls and drizzle each with oil.
6) Garnish with cheese and remaining basil and serve.

Effortless Chicken Stew

 Servings: 4　 **Cooking Time: 6 hours**　 **Preparation Time: 10 minutes**

Nutrition Information:

Calories per serving: 502; Carbohydrates: 15.9g;
Protein: 34.8g; Fat: 33.8g; Sugar: 7.3g; Sodium:
199mg; Fiber: 3.4g

Ingredients:

- 1 lb. boneless chicken breasts, chopped
- 1¼ lb. pearl onions, peeled
- 1-2 tbsp. fresh orange juice
- 1 cinnamon stick
- 10 peppercorns
- 2 bay leaves
- Pinch of allspice
- Salt and freshly ground black pepper, to taste
- 2 tbsp. tomato paste
- ½ C. extra-virgin olive oil
- 1 C. red cooking wine
- 1 C. water

Instructions:

1) In a slow cooker, place all the ingredients and stir to combine.
2) Set the slow cooker on "Low" and cook, covered for about 6 hours.
3) Serve hot.

Inspiring Spanish Beef Stew

Servings: 6   **Cooking Time: 5 hours 10 minutes**   **Preparation Time: 15 minutes**

Nutrition Information:

Calories per serving: 253; Carbohydrates: 18.6g;
Protein: 25.8g; Fat: 8.6g; Sugar: 5.3g; Sodium:
80mg; Fiber: 3.5g

Ingredients:

- 1 lb. beef stew meat, cubed
- Salt and freshly ground black pepper, to taste
- 1 tbsp. olive oil
- 2 red potatoes, cubed
- ½ C. Spanish onion, chopped
- ½ C. green olives, pitted
- 1 (14½-oz.) can diced tomatoes with juice
- 1 (12-oz.) jar tomato sauce

Instructions:

1) Season the beef with salt and black pepper evenly.
2) In a large skillet, heat the oil over medium heat and cook the beef for about 5 minutes
3) With a slotted spoon, transfer the beef into a slow cooker.
4) In the same skillet, add the onion and garlic and sauté for about 5 minutes.
5) Transfer the onion mixture into the slow cooker.
6) Add the remaining ingredients and stir to combine.
7) Set the slow cooker on "Low" and cook, covered for about 4-5 hours.
8) Serve hot.

Cretan Beef Stew

 **Servings: 6** **Cooking Time: 6 hours** **Preparation Time: 15 minutes**

Nutrition Information:

Calories per serving: 441; Carbohydrates: 13.6g;
Protein: 48.7g; Fat: 21.6g; Sugar: 7.1g; Sodium:
148mg; Fiber: 5.4g

Ingredients:	Instructions:

Ingredients:

- 2 lb. lean beef, cut into bite-sized cubes
- 2 onions, chopped
- 1 lb. eggplant, cubed
- 1 lb. zucchini, sliced
- 1 lb. tomatoes, chopped
- 1 tsp. dried thyme
- 2 tbsp. fresh mint, chopped
- Salt and freshly ground black pepper, to taste
- 5 tbsp. extra-virgin olive oil
- 5 C. water

Instructions:

1) In a slow cooker, place all the ingredients and stir to combine.
2) Set the slow cooker on "High" and cook, covered for about 6 hours.
3) Serve hot.

Brightened Beef Stew

 Servings: 10　 **Cooking Time: 10 hours**　 **Preparation Time: 15 minutes**

Nutrition Information:

Calories per serving: 368; Carbohydrates: 12.3g; Protein: 48.4g; Fat: 13.3g; Sugar: 5.7g; Sodium: 28mg; Fiber: 3.4g

Ingredients:

- 3 lb. beef stew meat
- 16 oz. sliced crimini mushrooms
- 1 large onion chopped
- 10 garlic cloves, minced
- 2 tbsp. dried rosemary
- 2 C. beef broth
- 2 (14½-oz.) cans diced tomatoes, drained
- 1 (15-oz.) can tomato sauce
- ½ C. balsamic vinegar
- 1 (6-oz.) can black olives, drained
- 1 (2-oz.) jar capers, drained
- 1 C. Parmesan cheese, shredded
- ½ C. fresh parsley, chopped

Instructions:

1) In a slow cooker, place all the ingredients except for cheese and parsley and stir to combine.
2) Set the slow cooker on "Low" and cook, covered for about 8-10 hours.
3) Serve hot with the garnishing of Parmesan cheese and parsley.

►► **Winter Dinner Lamb Stew**

 Servings: 8 **Cooking Time: 3 ¼ hours** **Preparation Time: 15 minutes**

Nutrition Information:

Calories per serving: 500; Carbohydrates: 12.5g; Protein: 55.5g; Fat: 26.7g; Sugar: 5.2g; Sodium: 480mg; Fiber: 3.8g

Ingredients:	Instructions:

Ingredients:

- 8 lamb shoulder chops
- Salt and freshly ground black pepper, to taste
- 3 tbsp. olive oil
- 8 garlic cloves, chopped
- 1 large onion, chopped
- 4 large plum tomatoes, chopped
- 2 C. chicken broth
- 1½ C. water
- 1½ lb. fresh chicory, chopped roughly
- ¼ C. fresh lemon juice
- ½ C. fresh dill, chopped

Instructions:

1) Season the lamb chops with salt and black pepper evenly. In a large skillet, heat 2 tbsp. of the oil over medium-high heat and sea the chops in 2 batches for about 3 minutes per side
2) With a slotted spoon, transfer the chops into a slow cooker.
3) In the same skillet, heat the remaining oil over medium heat and sauté the onion and garlic for about 5-6 minutes.
4) Add the tomatoes and cook for about 2-3 minutes, stirring frequently.
5) Add the broth and bring to a boil, scraping up the browned bits from the bottom.
6) Remove from the heat and transfer the mixture to the slow cooker.
7) Add the water and stir to combine.
8) Set the slow cooker on "High" and cook, covered for about 2 hours.
9) Uncover the slow cooker and spread the chicory on the top of the stew.
10) Set the slow cooker on "High" and cook, covered for about 1 hour, stirring 2-3 times.
11) Uncover the slow cooker and stir in the lemon juice and dill.
12) Serve hot.

►► Middle Eastern Comforting Stew

 **Servings: 6** **Cooking Time: 6 ¼ hours** **Preparation Time: 20 minutes**

Nutrition Information:

Calories per serving: 675; Carbohydrates: 61.7g;
Protein: 54.9g; Fat: 24.9g; Sugar: 14.8g; Sodium:
000mg; Fiber: 16.3g

Ingredients:	Instructions:

Ingredients:

- 2½ lb. lamb shoulder chops, cut into 1-inch cubes
- ½ tsp. dried mint
- 2 tsp. ground coriander
- 1 tsp. ground cumin
- ¼ tsp. ground turmeric
- ¼ tsp. red chili powder
- Salt and freshly ground black pepper, to taste
- 2 tbsp. olive oil, divided
- 1 medium onion, chopped
- 4 garlic cloves, minced
- 1 tbsp. fresh ginger, minced
- 1½ C. chicken broth
- 3 C. tomato sauce
- ½ C. tomatoes, chopped
- 1 (15-oz.) can chickpeas, drained and rinsed
- 2 C. baby potatoes, halved
- 1 C. fresh spinach, chopped

Instructions:

1) In a large bowl, add the lamb cubes, dried mint and spices and toss to coat well.
2) In a large skillet, heat 1 tbsp. of the oil over medium heat and sear the lamb cubes for about 6 minutes or until browned completely.
3) With a slotted spoon, transfer the lamb cubes into a slow cooker.
4) In the same skillet, heat the remaining oil over medium heat and sauté the onion, garlic and ginger for about 5-6 minutes.
5) Add the broth and tomato sauce and bring to a boil.
6) Transfer the onion mixture into the slow cooker with tomatoes, chickpeas and potatoes and stir to combine.
7) Set the slow cooker on "Low" and cook, covered for about 6 hours.
8) Uncover the slow cooker and stir in the spinach until wilted.
9) Serve hot.

▶▶ Richly Flavored Lamb Stew

 Servings: 6   **Cooking Time: 8 hours 50 minutes**   **Preparation Time: 15 minutes**

Nutrition Information:

Calories per serving: 435; Carbohydrates: 10.3g; Protein: 50.9g; Fat: 2-.4g; Sugar: 5g; Sodium: 675mg; Fiber: 2g

Ingredients:	Instructions:

Ingredients:

- 2 tbsp. olive oil
- 2¼ lb. lamb shoulder, cubed
- 2 onions, sliced
- 5 garlic cloves, crushed
- 1 tsp. fresh ginger, grated
- 1 tbsp. ground cumin
- 1 tbsp. ground coriander
- 1 tsp. ground cinnamon
- Pinch of saffron
- 1 tsp. lemon peel, grated
- 1 tbsp. tomato puree
- 2½ C. hot beef broth
- Salt and freshly ground black pepper, to taste
- 1 C. Kalamata olives, pitted
- 1 tbsp. honey
- 2 tbsp. fresh lemon juice

Instructions:

1) In a large skillet, heat 1 tbsp. of the 4-5 minutes or until browned completely.
2) With a slotted spoon, transfer the lamb cubes into a slow cooker.
3) In the same skillet, heat the remaining oil over medium heat and sauté the onion for about 4-6 minutes.
4) Add the garlic and ginger and sauté for about 1-2 minutes.
5) Add the spices, saffron, lemon peel and tomato puree and sauté for about 1-2 minutes.
6) Transfer the onion mixture into the slow cooker with broth, salt and black pepper and stir to combine.
7) Set the slow cooker on "Low" and cook, covered for about 6-8 hours.
8) Uncover the slow cooker and stir in the olives, honey and lemon juice.
9) Set the slow cooker on "High" and cook, covered for about 20-30 minutes.
10) Serve hot.

Sophisticated Pork Stew

 Servings: 6   **Cooking Time: 10 hours**   **Preparation Time: 15 minutes**

Nutrition Information:

Calories per serving: 354; Carbohydrates: 13.8g; Protein: 44.8g; Fat: 9.8g; Sugar: 5.7g; Sodium: 18mg; Fiber: 1.2g

Ingredients:	Instructions:

Ingredients:

- 2 lb. boneless pork loin, cut into 1-inch pieces
- 1/3 C. all-purpose flour
- ½ tsp. dried thyme
- ½ tsp. ground cinnamon
- 1 (14½-oz.) can chicken broth
- ¾ C. dry red wine
- 1 tbsp. balsamic vinegar
- 1 tbsp. honey
- 2 C. frozen pearl onions
- 4 oz. feta cheese, crumbled

Instructions:

1) In a bowl, add the pork cubes, flour, thyme and cinnamon and toss to coat well.
2) In a bowl, add broth, wine, vinegar and honey and beat until well combined.
3) In the bottom of a slow cooker, place the pork cubes and onions and top with broth mixture.
4) Set the slow cooker on "Low" and cook, covered for about 9-10 hours.
5) Serve hot with the topping of feta cheese.

Yummy Pork Stew

 Servings: 6   **Cooking Time: 5 hours**   **Preparation Time: 15 minutes**

Nutrition Information:

Calories per serving: 359; Carbohydrates: 7.3g;
Protein: 48.5g; Fat: 13.8g; Sugar: 3.5g; Sodium:
598mg; Fiber: 1.6g

Ingredients:

- 2 lb. pork tenderloins, cut into 2-inch pieces
- 2 large carrots, peeled and cut into ½-inch slices
- 2 celery stalks, chopped roughly
- 1 medium onion, chopped
- 1/3 C. olives, pitted
- 1/3 C. dried plums, pitted and chopped
- 4 garlic cloves, minced
- 2 bay leaves
- 1 fresh thyme sprig
- 1 fresh rosemary sprig
- Salt and freshly ground black pepper, to taste
- 2 tbsp. tomato paste
- 3 C. beef broth

Instructions:

1) In a slow cooker, place all the ingredients and stir to combine.
2) Set the slow cooker on "Low" and cook, covered for about 5-6 hours.
3) Uncover the slow cooker and discard the bay leaves and herb sprigs.
4) Serve hot.

Worth Trying Cod Stew

👥 **Servings: 8** 🕐 **Cooking Time: 3 hours 40 minutes** 🕐 **Preparation Time: 15 minutes**

Nutrition Information:

Calories per serving: 238; Carbohydrates: 14.6g;
Protein: 38.2g; Fat: 3g; Sugar: 4.3g; Sodium:
97mg; Fiber: 4.6g

Ingredients:

- 2 large leeks, cut into ¼-inch-thick slices
- 1½ lb. fennel bulb, chopped
- 2¼ lb. tomatoes, chopped
- 2 garlic cloves, chopped
- 8 fresh parsley sprigs
- 4 fresh thyme sprigs
- Salt and freshly ground black pepper, to taste
- ¼-½ C. dry white wine
- 2¾ lb. skinless cod fillets
- 2 tsp. extra-virgin olive oil

Instructions:

1) In a slow cooker, place all the ingredients except for cod and oil and stir to combine.
2) Set the slow cooker on "High" and cook, covered for about 3 hours.
3) Uncover the slow cooker and place fish on top of the stew.
4) Set the slow cooker on "High" and cook, covered for about 30-40 minutes.
5) Uncover the slow cooker and discard the herb sprigs.
6) Divide the stew into serving bowls.
7) Drizzle with oil and serve.

Busy Night Stew

 **Servings: 6** **Cooking Time: 4 hours** **Preparation Time: 20 minutes**

Nutrition Information:

Calories per serving: 286; Carbohydrates: 21.8g; Protein: 36.7g; Fat: 3.4g; Sugar: 5.4g; Sodium: 1200mg; Fiber: 3.7g

Ingredients:	Instructions:

Ingredients:

- 1 (28-oz.) can crushed tomatoes
- 4 C. vegetable broth
- ½ C. white wine
- 3 garlic cloves, minced
- 1 lb. baby potatoes, cut into bite-sized pieces
- ½ of medium onion, chopped
- 1 tsp. dried cilantro
- 1 tsp. dried thyme
- 1 tsp. dried basil
- ½ tsp. celery salt
- ¼ tsp. red pepper flakes
- Salt and freshly ground black pepper, to taste
- 1 lb. extra-large shrimp, peeled and deveined
- ½ lb. scallops
- ½ lb. crab legs

Instructions:

1) In a slow cooker., place all the ingredients except for seafood and stir to combine.
2) Set the slow cooker on "High" and cook, covered for about 2-3 hours.
3) Uncover the slow cooker and stir in the seafood.
4) Set the slow cooker on "High" and cook, covered for about 30-60 minutes.
5) Serve hot.

Saucier Vegetarian Stew

 Servings: 8   **Cooking Time: 4 hours 40 minutes** **Preparation Time: 20 minutes**

Nutrition Information:

Calories per serving: 230; Carbohydrates: 35.4g;
Protein: 8.9g; Fat: 7.4g; Sugar: 12g; Sodium:
7mg; Fiber: 13.5g

Ingredients:

- 1 oz. dried porcini mushrooms
- 3 C. hot water
- 3 lb. eggplants, halved lengthwise
- 3 tbsp. extra-virgin olive oil, divided
- 2 large onions, sliced thinly
- 6 garlic cloves, minced
- 2 tsp. dried oregano, crumbled
- 1 bay leaf
- 1 small (1-inch) cinnamon stick
- Salt and freshly ground black pepper, to taste
- 1 C. dried chickpeas, soaked overnight and drained
- 1 (28-oz.) can whole tomatoes, drained and chopped roughly
- ¼ C. fresh parsley, chopped

Instructions:

1) Preheat the oven to 400 degrees F.
2) In a bowl, soak the dried mushrooms in hot water for about 30 minutes.
3) Through a sieve, strain the mushrooms, reserving the soaking liquid in a bowl.
4) Then, chop the mushrooms finely.
5) Meanwhile, peel eggplants, if desired, and cut in half lengthwise.
6) Brush the cut sides of eggplants with 2 tbsp. of the oil.
7) Arrange the eggplant halves onto a rimmed baking sheet, cut-side down.
8) Roast for about 25 minutes.
9) Remove from the oven and set the eggplants aside to cool slightly.
10) Then, cut the eggplants into 1-inch cubes and transfer into a slow cooker.
11) Meanwhile, in a large skillet, heat the remaining oil over medium heat and sauté the onions for about 4-5 minutes.
12) Add the mushrooms, garlic, oregano, cinnamon stick, bay leaf, salt and black pepper and sauté for about 1 minute.
13) Add the reserved soaking liquid and chickpeas and bring to a boil.
14) Cook for about 5 minutes, stirring occasionally.
15) Remove from the heat and transfer the chickpeas mixture into the slow cooker.
16) With a spoon, stir the chickpeas mixture with the eggplant.
17) Set the slow cooker on "High" and cook, covered for about 4 hours.
18) Uncover the slow cooker and discard the cinnamon stick and bay leaf.
19) Stir in the tomatoes and parsley and serve.

Vegetables Loaded Stew

 **Servings: 6** **Cooking Time: 6 hours** **Preparation Time: 15 minutes**

Nutrition Information:

Calories per serving: 137; Carbohydrates: 15.3g;
Protein: 5.9g; Fat: 7g; Sugar: 8.4g; Sodium:
611mg; Fiber: 5.5g

Ingredients:

- 2 tbsp. extra-virgin olive oil
- 4 garlic cloves, chopped
- 1 medium red onion, chopped
- 1 small eggplant, chopped
- 1 medium red bell pepper, seeded and chopped
- 1/3 C. Kalamata olives, pitted and chopped
- 2 (15-oz.) cans diced tomatoes
- 4 C. vegetable broth
- ½ tsp. dried parsley
- ½ tsp. dried oregano
- 1 tsp. red pepper flakes, crushed
- Salt and freshly ground black pepper, to taste
- 4 tbsp. fresh chives, minced

Instructions:

1) In a slow cooker, place all the ingredients except for chives and stir to combine.
2) Set the slow cooker on "Low" and cook, covered for about 4-6 hours.
3) Serve hot with the garnishing of chives.

Wicked-Easy Stew

 Servings: 6   **Cooking Time: 7 ½ hours**   **Preparation Time: 15 minutes**

Nutrition Information:

Calories per serving: 238; Carbohydrates: 35.1g;
Protein: 8.9g; Fat: 8.2g; Sugar: 5.1g; Sodium:
30mg; Fiber: 7g

Ingredients:

- 2 (14-oz.) cans fire-roasted diced tomatoes
- 1 C. onion, chopped
- ¾ C. carrot, peeled and chopped
- 4 garlic cloves, minced
- 1 tsp. dried oregano
- ½ tsp. red pepper flakes, crushed
- Salt and freshly ground black pepper, to taste
- 3 C. low-sodium vegetable broth
- 1 (15-oz.) can chickpeas, rinsed, drained and divided
- 8 C. fresh kale, tough ribs removed and chopped
- 1 tbsp. fresh lemon juice
- 3 tbsp. extra-virgin olive oil

Instructions:

1) In a slow cooker, place the tomatoes, onion, carrot, garlic, oregano, red pepper flakes, salt, black pepper and broth and stir to combine.
2) Set the slow cooker on "Low" and cook, covered for about 6 hours.
3) Uncover the slow cooker and transfer ¼ C. of the cooking liquid into a small bowl.
4) In the bowl with cooking liquid, add 2 tbsp. of chickpeas and with a fork, mash until smooth.
5) In the slow cooker, add the mashed chickpeas, kale, lemon juice and remaining chickpeas and stir to combine.
6) Set the slow cooker on "Low" and cook, covered for about 30 minutes.
7) Transfer the soup into serving bowls and drizzle each with oil.
8) Serve immediately.

Pretty Tasty Stew

 **Servings: 4** **Cooking Time: 8 hours 5 minutes** **Preparation Time: 15 minutes**

Nutrition Information:

Calories per serving: 353; Carbohydrates: 56.4g;
Protein: 12.3g; Fat: 9.2g; Sugar: 7.3g; Sodium:
681mg; Fiber: 11.7g

Ingredients:

- 2 tbsp. olive oil
- 1 large carrot, peeled and sliced
- 3 shallots, chopped
- 2 garlic cloves, minced
- 1 lb. small red potatoes, quartered
- 1 red bell pepper, seeded and chopped
- 9 oz. frozen artichoke hearts
- 1 (14½-oz.) can diced tomatoes
- 1½ C. cooked chickpeas
- 1 tsp. fresh thyme, minced
- 1 tsp. fresh oregano, minced
- 1 large bay leaf
- Salt and freshly ground black pepper, to taste
- 1/3 C. dry white wine
- 1½ C. vegetable broth

Instructions:

1) In a skillet, heat the oil over medium heat and sauté the carrots, shallots and garlic for about 4-5 minutes.
2) Remove from the heat and transfer the carrot mixture into a slow cooker.
3) Add the remaining ingredients and stir to combine.
4) Set the slow cooker on "Low" and cook, covered for about 6-8 hours.
5) Serve hot.

VEGETARIAN RECIPES

Ideal Cauliflower Mash

 Servings: 6   **Cooking Time: 3 hours**   **Preparation Time: 15 minutes**

Nutrition Information:

Calories per serving: 105; Carbohydrates: 5.4g;
Protein: 5.3g; Fat: 7g; Sugar: 2.7g; Sodium:
601mg; Fiber: 1.5g

Ingredients:

- 1 head cauliflower, cut into bite-sized pieces
- 5 garlic cloves, smashed
- 4 C. vegetable broth
- 1/3 C. Greek yogurt
- 3 tbsp. butter, cut into cubes
- 2 tbsp. fresh chives, chopped
- 1 tbsp. fresh parsley, chopped
- 1 tbsp. fresh rosemary, chopped
- 1 tsp. garlic powder
- Salt and freshly ground black pepper, to taste

Instructions:

1) In a slow cooker, place the cauliflower, garlic and broth and stir to combine.
2) Set the slow cooker on "High" and cook, covered for about 2½-3 hours.
3) Uncover the slow cooker and through a strainer, drain the cauliflower and garlic, reserving ½ C. of the broth.
4) Transfer the cauliflower into a bowl and with a potato masher, mash the cauliflower slightly.
5) Add the yogurt, butter and desired amount of reserved broth and mash until smooth.
6) Add the herbs, garlic powder, salt and black pepper and stir to combine.
7) Serve warm.

Easy Mashed Potatoes

 Servings: 10 **Cooking Time: 2 ½ hours** **Preparation Time: 15 minutes**

Nutrition Information:

Calories per serving: 148; Carbohydrates: 21.9g; Protein: 3.8g; Fat: 5.7g; Sugar: 3.8g; Sodium: 8mg; Fiber: 2.6g

Ingredients:

- 6 medium red potatoes, cut into ½-inch thick slices
- ½ C. scallions, chopped
- 1 tbsp. fresh oregano, chopped
- 2 tbsp. extra-virgin olive oil
- 2 tbsp. fresh lemon juice
- 2 oz. feta cheese, crumbled
- ½ C. half-and-half
- ¼ C. fresh parsley, chopped

Instructions:

1) In a slow cooker, place the potatoes, scallions, oregano oil and lemon juice and mix well.
2) Set the slow cooker on "High" and cook, covered for about 2½ hours.
3) Uncover the slow cooker.
4) Add the feta cheese and half-and-half and with a spoon until creamy.
5) Serve warm with the garnishing of parsley.

►► Meat-Free Mushroom StrOganoff

👨‍👩‍👧 **Servings: 3**   🕐 **Cooking Time: 5 hours**   🕐 **Preparation Time: 10 minutes**

Nutrition Information:

Calories per serving: 87; Carbohydrates: 12.2g; Protein: 8.6g; Fat:2.1g; Sugar: 5.2g; Sodium: 323mg; Fiber: 3.4g

Ingredients:	Instructions:

Ingredients:

- 1¼ lb. fresh mushrooms, halved
- 1 onion, sliced thinly
- 3 garlic cloves, minced
- 2 tsp. smoked paprika
- 1 C. vegetable broth
- 1 tbsp. sour cream
- Salt and freshly ground black pepper, to taste
- 4 tbsp. fresh parsley, chopped

Instructions:

1) In a slow cooker, place the mushrooms, onion, garlic, paprika and broth and stir to combine.
2) Set the slow cooker on "High" and cook, covered for about 4 hours.
3) Uncover the slow cooker and stir in the sour cream, salt and black pepper.
4) Serve with the garnishing of parsley.

Brussels Sprout

 Servings: 6   **Cooking Time: 4 hours 10 minutes**   **Preparation Time: 10 minutes**

Nutrition Information:

Calories per serving: 169; Carbohydrates: 17g; Protein: 6.5g; Fat: 9.9g; Sugar: 6.3g; Sodium: 50mg; Fiber: 5.7g

Ingredients:

- ½ C. balsamic vinegar
- 2 tbsp. brown sugar
- 2 lb. Brussels sprouts, trimmed and halved
- 2 tbsp. olive oil
- Salt and freshly ground black pepper, to taste
- 2 tbsp. unsalted butter, cubed
- ¼ C. Parmesan cheese, shredded

Instructions:

1) For balsamic reduction: in a small pan, add the vinegar and brown sugar over medium heat and bring to a gentle boil.
2) Cook for about 6-8 minutes, stirring frequently.
3) Remove from the heat and set aside to cool.
4) In a slow cooker, place the brussels sprouts, olive oil, salt and black pepper, and stir to combine.
5) Place the butter cubes on top.
6) Set the slow cooker on "Low" and cook, covered for about 3-4 hours.
7) Uncover the slow cooker and transfer the brussels sprouts into a bowl.
8) Drizzle with balsamic reduction and serve immediately with the topping of Parmesan.

▶ ▶ Garden Fresh Veggies Ratatouille

 Servings: 8 **Cooking Time: 6 hours** **Preparation Time: 15 minutes**

Nutrition Information:

Calories per serving: 125; Carbohydrates: 11.5g;
Protein: 2.7g; Fat: 8.9g; Sugar: 6g; Sodium:
38mg; Fiber: 4.3g

Ingredients:	Instructions:

Ingredients:

- 1 C. fresh basil
- 3 garlic cloves, minced
- 1/3 C. olive oil
- 2 tbsp. white wine vinegar
- 2 tbsp. fresh lemon juice
- 2 tbsp. tomato paste
- Salt, to taste
- 2 medium zucchini, cut into small chunks
- 2 medium summer squash, cut into small chunks
- 1 small eggplant, cut into small chunks
- 1 large white onion, cut into small chunks
- 2 C. cherry tomatoes

Instructions:

1) In a food processor, add the basil, garlic, oil, vinegar, lemon juice, tomato paste and salt and pulse until smooth.
2) In the bottom of a slow cooker, place all the vegetables and top with the pureed mixture evenly.
3) Set the slow cooker on "Low" and cook, covered for about 5-6 hours.
4) Serve hot.

 # Colorful Veggie Combo

 Servings: 4 **Cooking Time: 3 hours** **Preparation Time: 15 minutes**

Nutrition Information:

Calories per serving: 203; Carbohydrates: 23.6g;
Protein: 8.1g; Fat: 190.3; Sugar: 13.4g; Sodium:
73mg; Fiber: 7.8g

Ingredients:

- 1 tbsp. olive oil
- 1 lb. eggplant, peeled and cut into 1-inch cubes
- 1 small zucchini, chopped
- 1 small yellow squash, chopped
- 1 small orange bell pepper, seeded and chopped
- 1 small yellow bell pepper, seeded and chopped
- 1 large red onion, chopped
- 4 plum tomatoes, chopped
- 4 garlic cloves, minced
- 2 tsp. dried basil
- Salt and freshly ground black pepper, to taste
- 4 oz. feta cheese, crumbled

Instructions:

1) In a slow cooker, place all the ingredients except for cheese and stir to combine.
2) Set the slow cooker on "High" and cook, covered for about 3 hours.
3) Serve hot with the topping of feta cheese.

▶▶ Friday Dinner Veggie Meal

 Servings: 6   **Cooking Time: 4 hours**   **Preparation Time: 15 minutes**

Nutrition Information:

Calories per serving: 181; Carbohydrates: 27.1g;
Protein: 10.4g; Fat:3.; Sugar: 6.3g; Sodium:
723mg; Fiber: 9.3g

Ingredients:	Instructions:

Ingredients:

- 2 (15-oz.) cans cannellini beans, rinsed and drained
- 1 (14.5-oz.) can diced tomatoes with basil, garlic and oregano
- 1 C. zucchini, chopped
- 1 C. red bell pepper, seeded and chopped
- ½ C. Kalamata olives, pitted and halved
- 2 garlic cloves, minced
- ¼ C. fresh parsley, chopped
- Freshly ground black pepper, to taste
- 2 tbsp. balsamic vinegar
- 2 tbsp. fresh lemon juice
- 1 C. vegetable broth
- ¼ C. feta cheese, crumbled

Instructions:

1) In a slow cooker, place all the ingredients except for cheese and stir to combine.
2) Set the slow cooker on "Low" and cook, covered for about 4 hours.
3) Serve hot with the topping of feta cheese.

 # Deliciously Spicy Chickpeas

 Servings: 6   **Cooking Time: 6 hours**   **Preparation Time: 15 minutes**

Nutrition Information:

Calories per serving: 316; Carbohydrates: 40.5g;
Protein: 9.3g; Fat: 14.5g; Sugar: 13.3g; Sodium:
32mg; Fiber: 10.6g

Ingredients:	Instructions:

Ingredients:

- 8 oz. dried chickpeas, soaked overnight and drained
- ½ C. extra-virgin olive oil
- 2 onions, chopped
- 1 (28-oz.) can crushed tomatoes
- 2 carrots, peeled and chopped
- 2 medium potatoes, chopped
- 3 garlic cloves, minced
- ½ bunch fresh cilantro, stemmed and chopped
- ½ bunch fresh parsley, stemmed and chopped
- ½ tsp. ground turmeric
- ½ tsp. paprika
- ½ tsp. ground cumin
- ¼ tsp. ground coriander
- ¼ tsp. ground cinnamon
- ¼ tsp. curry powder
- ¼ tsp. red pepper flakes, crushed
- Salt and freshly ground black pepper, to taste
- 1 tbsp. honey
- 3 C. water

Instructions:

1) In a slow cooker, place all the ingredients and stir to combine.
2) Set the slow cooker on "High" and cook, covered for about 6 hours.
3) Serve hot.

Meatless Dinner Meal

 **Servings: 6** **Cooking Time: 4 hours 5 minutes** **Preparation Time: 15 minutes**

Nutrition Information:

Calories per serving: 248; Carbohydrates: 39.6g;
Protein: 9.3g; Fat: 6.9g; Sugar: 2.8g; Sodium:
823mg; Fiber: 8.4g

Ingredients:

- 1 tbsp. olive oil
- 1 sweet onion, sliced thinly
- 3 garlic cloves, minced
- 30 oz. canned chickpeas, rinsed and drained
- 1 zucchini, chopped
- 1 C. roasted red peppers, chopped
- 1 C. olives, pitted
- 1 C. vegetable broth
- 1 tbsp. capers
- 1 tsp. dried rosemary
- 1 tsp. dried oregano
- 1 tsp. dried thyme
- 1 bay leaf
- Salt and freshly ground black pepper, to taste

Instructions:

1) In a skillet, heat the oil over medium-high heat and sauté the onions and garlic for about 4-5 minutes.
2) Transfer the onion into the cooker with remaining ingredients and stir to combine.
3) Set the slow cooker on "Low" and cook, covered for about 4 hours.
4) Serve hot.

 # Italian Veggie Dinner Casserole

 Servings: 5 **Cooking Time: 8 hours** **Preparation Time: 15 minutes**

Nutrition Information:

Calories per serving: 506; Carbohydrates: 87.1g; Protein: 25.7g; Fat: 8.4g; Sugar: 22.8g; Sodium: 59mg; Fiber: 21.2g

Ingredients:

- 1 (15-oz.) can chickpeas, rinsed and drained
- 3 medium carrots, peeled and sliced
- 1 medium onion, chopped
- 1 (28-oz.) can diced tomatoes with juice
- 2 garlic cloves, chopped finely
- 1 (6-oz.) can Italian-style tomato paste
- 1 C. water
- 2 tsp. sugar
- 1 tsp. Italian seasoning
- Salt and freshly ground black pepper, to taste
- 1½ C. frozen cut green beans, thawed
- 1 C. uncooked elbow macaroni
- ½ C. Parmesan cheese, shredded

Instructions:

1) In a slow cooker, place all the ingredients except for green beans, macaroni and parmesan cheese and stir to combine.
2) Set the slow cooker on "Low" and cook, covered for about 6-8 hours.
3) Uncover the slow cooker and stir in the green beans and macaroni.
4) Set the slow cooker on "High" and cook, covered for about 20 minutes.
5) Top with cheese and serve hot.

Perfect Rice Platter

 Servings: 6 **Cooking Time: 2 hours 10 minutes** **Preparation Time: 15 minutes**

Nutrition Information:

Calories per serving: 378; Carbohydrates: 57.9g; Protein: 11.6g; Fat: 10.8g; Sugar: 4.5g; Sodium: 906mg; Fiber: 2.5g

Ingredients:

- 2 (14-oz.) cans vegetable broth
- Water, as required
- 1 tbsp. plus 1 tsp. olive oil
- 2 C. converted rice
- 1 onion, chopped finely
- 1 tbsp. garlic, minced
- 1 tsp. Greek seasoning
- 1 tsp. dried oregano
- 1 green bell pepper, seeded and chopped finely
- 1 red bell pepper, seeded and chopped finely
- ¾ C. Kalamata olives, pitted and sliced
- 1 C. feta cheese, crumbled
- ¼ C. scallion, sliced
- 2 tbsp. fresh lemon juice
- Salt and freshly ground black pepper, to taste

Instructions:

1) In a bowl, add the broth and enough water to make the liquid about 4 cups. Set aside.
2) In a large heavy-bottomed skillet, heat 1 tbsp. of the oil over medium heat and sauté the rice for about 2-3 minutes or until browned.
3) Transfer the browned rice into a slow cooker.
4) In the same skillet, heat the remaining oil over medium heat and sauté the onions for about 4-5 minutes.
5) Add the garlic, Greek seasoning and oregano and sauté for about 1-2 minutes.
6) Transfer the onion mixture into the slow cooker with the rice.
7) Set the slow cooker on "High" and cook, covered for about 1½ hours.
8) Uncover the slow cooker and stir in the bell peppers.
9) Set the slow cooker on "High" and cook, covered for about 15 minutes.
10) Uncover the slow cooker and stir in the olives and feta.
11) Set the slow cooker on "High" and cook, covered for about 15 minutes.
12) Uncover the slow cooker and stir in the lemon juice, salt and black pepper.
13) Garnish with scallion and serve.

 # Familiar Mediterranean Dish

 Servings: 6 **Cooking Time: 4 hours** **Preparation Time: 15 minutes**

Nutrition Information:

Calories per serving: 536; Carbohydrates: 78.5g;
Protein: 23.2g; Fat: 16.1g; Sugar: 11.1g; Sodium:
25mg; Fiber: 17.4g

Ingredients:	Instructions:

Ingredients:

- 2¼ C. unsalted vegetable broth
- 1½ C. uncooked quinoa, rinsed
- 1 (15½-oz.) can chickpeas, drained and rinsed
- 1 C. red onions, sliced
- 2 garlic cloves, minced
- 2½ tbsp. olive oil
- Salt, to taste
- 2 tsp. fresh lemon juice
- ½ C. roasted red bell peppers, drained and chopped
- 4 C. fresh baby arugula
- 12 kalamata olives, pitted and halved lengthwise
- 2 oz. feta cheese, crumbled
- 2 tbsp. fresh oregano, chopped

Instructions:

1) In a slow cooker, place the broth, quinoa, chickpeas, onions, garlic, 1½ tsp. of the oil and salt and stir to combine.
2) Set the slow cooker on "Low" and cook, covered for about 3-4 hours.
3) Meanwhile, in a bowl, add the lemon juice, remaining oil and some salt and mix well.
4) Uncover the slow cooker and with a fork, fluff the quinoa mixture.
5) In the slow cooker, add the olive oil mixture, bell peppers and arugula and gently, stir to combine.
6) Over the pot for about 5 minutes before serving.
7) Garnish with the olives, feta cheese and oregano and serve.

Artichoke Pasta

 Servings: 4   **Cooking Time: 8 hours**   **Preparation Time: 15 minutes**

Nutrition Information:

Calories per serving: 479; Carbohydrates: 82.2g;
Protein: 20.8g; Fat: 10.4g; Sugar: 10.5g; Sodium:
407mg; Fiber: 14.8g

Ingredients:

- 3 (14½-oz.) cans diced tomatoes with basil, oregano, and garlic
- 2 (14-oz.) cans artichoke hearts, drained and quartered
- 6 garlic cloves, minced
- ½ C. whipping cream
- 12 oz. dried fettuccine pasta
- ¼ C. pimiento-stuffed green olives
- ¼ c. feta cheese, crumbled

Instructions:

1) Drain the juices from two of the cans of diced tomatoes.
2) In a greased slow cooker, place the drained and undrained tomatoes alongside the artichoke hearts and garlic and mix well.
3) Set the slow cooker on "Low" and cook, covered for about 6-8 hours.
4) Meanwhile, in a large pan of the salted boiling water, cook the pasta for about 8-10 minutes or according to the package's directions.
5) Drain the pasta and rinse under cold running water
6) Uncover the slow cooker and stir in the whipping cream.
7) Divide the pasta onto serving plates and top with artichoke sauce.
8) Garnish with olives and cheese and serve.

Ingenious Veggie Lasagna

 Servings: 8   **Cooking Time: 2 hours**   **Preparation Time: 20 minutes**

Nutrition Information:

Calories per serving: 289; Carbohydrates: 37.1g; Protein: 18.8g; Fat: 8.2g; Sugar: 5.8g; Sodium: 69mg; Fiber: 3.3g

Ingredients:	Instructions:

Ingredients:

- 1 (5-oz.) package baby spinach, chopped roughly
- 3 large portobello mushroom caps, gills removed, halved and sliced thinly
- 1 small zucchini, quartered lengthwise and sliced thinly
- 1 (16-oz.) container part-skim ricotta cheese
- 1 large egg
- 1 (28-oz.) can diced tomatoes
- 1 (28-oz.) can crushed tomatoes
- 3 garlic cloves, minced
- Pinch of red pepper flakes, crushed
- 15 uncooked whole-wheat lasagna noodles
- 3 C. part-skim mozzarella, shredded and divided

Instructions:

1) In a large bowl, add the spinach, zucchini, ricotta cheese and egg and mix well.
2) In another bowl, add both cans of tomatoes with juice, garlic and red pepper flakes and mix well.
3) In the bottom of a generously greased slow cooker, place about 1½ C. of the tomato mixture evenly.
4) Place 5 lasagna noodles over the tomato mixture, overlapping them slightly and breaking them to fit in the pot.
5) Spread half of the ricotta mixture over the noodles.
6) Now, place about 1½ C. of the tomato mixture and sprinkle with 1 C. of the mozzarella.
7) Repeat the layers twice.
8) Set the slow cooker on "High" and cook, covered for about 2 hours.
9) Uncover the slow cooker and sprinkle with the remaining mozzarella cheese.
10) Immediately, cover the cooker for about 10 minutes before serving.

▶ ▶Best-Ever Homemade Hummus

 Servings: 10 **Cooking Time: 4 hours** **Preparation Time: 15 minutes**

Nutrition Information:

Calories per serving: 190; Carbohydrates: 19.7g;
Protein: 6.9g; Fat: 10.1g; Sugar: 3.3g; Sodium:
16mg; Fiber: 5.8g

Ingredients:	Instructions:

Ingredients:

- 1½ C. dried chickpeas, rinsed
- 2-3 C. water
- 2 garlic cloves, peeled
- ¼ C. olive oil
- 2 tbsp. fresh lemon juice
- ¼ C. tahini

Instructions:

1) In a slow cooker, place the chickpeas and water.
2) Set the slow cooker on "High" and cook, covered for about 4 hours.
3) Uncover the slow cooker and drain the chickpeas, reserving about 1/3 C. of the cooking liquid cooking and remaining ingredients and pulse until smooth.
4) Transfer the hummus into a bowl and refrigerator before serving.

CPSIA information can be obtained
at www.ICGtesting.com
Printed in the USA
LVHW061456010221
677982LV00013B/446